M. P. Robinson

MW00443153

AMX-30
Char de Bataille
1966–2006
vol. I

This book is dedicated to the memory of Jacques About, France olympian, educator, our cousin and friend.

KAGERO

Introduction

The AMX-30B *Char de Bataille de Trente Tonnes*, fondly known as the X-trente to its crews, was for many years the main weapon of the French armoured corps. Until it began to be replaced in some units by the AMX-30B2 in 1982, it was never known as anything but the AMX-30 to the men who used it. A wide range of special purpose variants were produced on the AMX-30B chassis, vehicles still in service today alongside a small number of gun tanks. The AMX-30 design, throughout its career, stayed true to its design philosophy; it remained a fast, heavily armed and lightly armoured tank. Like some contemporary designs, its early years were not without teething troubles and the AMX-30B was a spartan design in many ways, lacking gun stabilisation and with a fragile transmission. This volume's text treats the development of the AMX-30 series and its early years in service, while its photographic content is focused on the AMX-30B, its origins, and its service life. A subsequent volume on the later years of the AMX-30's service, with photo coverage focused on the AMX-30B2, is in preparation.

The Author would like to thank the following people

I thank Tomasz Basarabowicz for his help with organizing this project with Kagero. I would like to express my sincere gratitude to Pierre Delattre, Olivier Carneau, and Claude Balmefrezol who encouraged my research and ensured I was put in touch with some of France's experts on the AMX-30 series. My gratitude to Thomas Seignon, Christophe Legrand, Noel Legros, Jacques Maillard and Roger Dannacker for their contributions cannot be stated enough. Steven Zaloga, Julie Ludmann, Guy Gibeau, Luis Pitarch Carrion, Triantafyllos Metsovitis, Francis Cany, Jonathan Cany, Phillipe Besson, Marcel Toulon, Stelios Markides, Paul Baron, Zurich, and Lionel Gonnet all must be thanked for their contribution of information, insight, research material, photographs and encouragement. The author would also like to salute the efforts of Xavier Lena, Jean-Francois Brilliant, Pierre Piveteau and the many other French armoured enthusiasts and historians who have made researching this work possible by their kind help or by maintaining websites that have enabled discussion and study of these vehicles. Lastly, I must thank my wife Nisa and our children Leif, Owyn, Alexandria, Griffin and Thor for their patience in preparing this volume.

M.P. Robinson

AMX-30. Char de Bataille 1966–2006. Vol. I • M.P. Robinson • First edition • LUBLIN 2014

© All English Language Rights Reserved. With the exception of quoting brief passages for the purposes of review, no part of this publication may be reproduced without prior written permission from the Publisher. Nazwa serii zastrzeżona w UP RP • ISBN 978-83-62878-99-4

Editors: M.P. Robinson, Tomasz Basarabowicz • Color profiles: Sławomir Zajączkowski
• Design: KAGERO STUDIO, Marcin Wachowicz, Łukasz Maj

Oficyna Wydawnicza KAGERO
Akacjowa 100, Turka, os. Borek, 20-258 Lublin 62, Poland, phone/fax: (+48) 81 501 21 05
www.kagero.pl • e-mail: kagero@kagero.pl, marketing@kagero.pl
w w w . k a g e r o . p l

The AMX-50 was the first medium tank designed in France after the war, and it included a very advanced turret concept and a hull influenced by the German Panther. Great things were expected of the AMX-50 and it evolved into a heavy tank rather than the medium tank first built in 1949. Its failure to be adopted in 1956 was a reflection of France's changing military priorities as much as it was a consequence of American largesse. Testing of the later versions continued until 1958. [Thomas Seignon]

The AMX-30

The AMX-30 was the French Army's main battle tank (or *Char de Bataille*) for the second half of the Cold War. In June 1966 as the first production AMX-30 rolled off the production line, the French arms industry was an innovative and successful armoured vehicle design, production and marketing center. France had a relatively strong economy and a large degree of government control and subsidization in its strategic industries.

Great things were expected of the AMX-30 design, which had been conceived as a weapon to arm the armoured forces of Western Europe. The AMX-30 did not achieve the degree of export success met by its lighter predecessor for a variety of reasons, but the battle tank and its derivatives have ultimately served the French army for over 46 years. The AMX-30 series was France's most significant land weapon system for two generations and represented a significantly different approach to tank design than most of its western contemporaries.

On the 6th of June 1963 the AMX-30 *préserie* (often called AMX-30A) vehicles were presented to the army at Mailly (between Troyes and Rheims in eastern France). These two photos are taken from the original pamphlet given out at the event by DTAT, and depict Prototype 2. Note how the NBC system seen on production vehicles is absent from the turret rear. [Thomas Seignon]

While the general layout later adopted for the AMX-30 B is easy to find in its predecessor, the prototype and *préserie* vehicles differed in many details from the production AMX-30B (features that took some three years to evolve to the familiar standard of the AMX-30B). The most visible changes were the turret stowage cages and the replacement of the original low-profile S-470 cupola with the TOP 7 (*Tourelleau d'Observation Panoramique N° 7*). Studies of a cupola mounted 12.7mm machine gun and of a cupola mounted 20mm cannon were abandoned early on, but both of these powerful weapons were employed as co-axial armament on the production AMX-30B. [Thomas Seignon]

Cover sheet for the pamphlet issued by DTAT at the time of the official presentation of the AMX-30 to the French Army. We can see that the designation of AMX-30A was used by the manufacturer. It is dated June 6th 1963. [Thomas Seignon]

Part of the technical information included in the AMX-30A pamphlet of June 6th 1963, which explains (amongst other things) that the *préserie* vehicles were armoured to resist 20mm armour piercing rounds and stressing the sloped layout of the armour (as opposed to its thickness) as the basis of the tank's protection. These were the AMX-30 pre-production vehicles that were evaluated against the pre-production Leopard 1 later in 1963. [Thomas Seignon]

The second sheet from the technical information included in the 1963 pamphlet indicates that the cupola mounted armament on production tanks (at least as foreseen in 1963) was going to be a 20mm cannon. At the time weapons of this type were only beginning to be studied as the main armament for infantry armoured personnel carriers. By the time the AMX-30B entered series production in 1966, its' TOP-7 cupola mounted the ANF-1 7.62mm machine gun, a far more practical weapon for a tank commander. [Thomas Seignon]

A DTAT photograph of what must be one of the two final pre-production vehicles, which were supposed to define the series production vehicles. The production tanks evolved substantially in terms of turret casting, cupola type and hull construction before actual production began late in 1965. We can see some of the definitive signs all the same: the turret baskets on the sides of the turret and the thermal sleeve became standard features. This one mounts the S-470 cupola seen on the *présérie* vehicles evaluated against the pre-production Leopard in 1963. [MP Robinson]

Why a 30-Ton Tank?

Between the early 1950s and 1966, France had arguably already succeeded beyond any other European nation in two domains of the market for land warfare systems: creating light armoured vehicles with exceptional firepower, and the development of guided antitank missile technology. The AMX-13

light tank was the epitome of how successful the French tank design philosophy could be. The French government had every aspiration to become the arsenal of Europe by extending this expertise into the production of battle tanks for their European allies and for export markets.

The expertise accumulated in the AMX-13 program became the guiding force for the design and production parameters of

A very proud young crew from the 503e RCC in the aftermath of the successful parade debut of the AMX-30B on July 14th 1967 in Paris. The 503e RCC was represented by 26 new AMX-30s, which advanced impressively down the *Champs Élysées* behind their regimental standard. [Noel Legros]

The *14 Juillet* parade on the *Champs Élysées* on July 14th 1968. The regiment is again the 503e RCC, the regiment which first deployed the AMX-30B and later the AMX-30B2. By 1968 the 501e RCC was also in the process of re-equipping with the AMX-30, as were the ABC's training establishment. [Noel Legros]

the *Char de Bataille* AMX-30. The *Char de Bataille* or Battle Tank concept adopted in France specified a 30 ton medium tank design for the role equivalent to the Main Battle Tank seen in other NATO armies. The choice of a lighter tank design than contemporary armies might have found ideal came because of the failure of earlier French designs of the 45 to 60 ton class. French success in combining relatively powerful guns on light chassis drove French design philosophy towards a lighter battle tank as much as factors like cost did.

The AMX-30's development was heavily influenced by the failure of previous attempts to create a viable French medium tank design in late 1940s and early 1950s. Attempts to revive the French tank industry in the period following 1945 were crippled by the lack of necessary funding and by a lack of modern

Celebration of the *St Georges* 1968: M47s of the *1e Régiment de Cuirassiers* and their crews during inspection. The M47 was a stalwart tank that served France adequately for much of the 1950s and 1960s, and whose arrival led in no small part to the cancelation of the AMX-50 project. [Paul Baron]

At the dawn of 1970, before the arrival of the first AMX-30, the general commanding the 1e Division Blindée inspects the crews of the M47 Pattons of the 1er RC, based at St Wendel in West Germany. The markings are quite intricate and the crews are in their dress uniforms, a far cry from the practical attire of life on a tank. Note that each Patton by then only had a 4 man crew, perhaps in preparation for the arrival of the AMX-30. [Thomas Seignon].

designs. Tanks in France had traditionally been built by both the government arsenals and by the private sector heavy engineering firms, a trend which gradually shifted towards a government dominated enterprise by the 1950s, a position consolidated in the 1960s and 1970s, during which time tank design by French private sector companies ceased.

The first step towards government domination of France's tank manufacture came before the war ended, the ARL-44.

The ARL-44 marked an important change in how tank construction was coordinated in France, with government control in the design and production of the vehicle. The ARL-44 was unfortunately a technical anachronism in most respects, comparing unfavourably to contemporary designs like the M26, the Centurion and the T44. The vehicle took nearly four years to reach operational status and its design was not representative of what the French Army required or wanted in a medium tank.

A view of the entrance to the 501e RCC's base in the late 1960s from a period postcard. The M47s seen here were probably gate guardians. The M47 was a dependable tank but was seen by the French as a vehicle with too little firepower for its weight. [C. Legrand]

An AMX-13 preserved at Thierville on the base of the *1e-2e Régiment de Chasseurs*. The AMX-13 was a big success on the export market and served in the French Army until the mid-1980s. [Francis Cany]

The Leopard 1 arose from the same specification as the AMX-30. In 1962 a special trials peloton was raised at Rambouillet from experienced officers and NCOs of the *Arme Blindée Cavalerie* under the command of three officers: Capitaine Gamache, Lieutenant Peloux, and Sous-Lieutenant Roger Dannacker. Six *preserie* AMX-30 vehicles and 7 crews were available to the trials team though only 5 tanks were trialled versus the Leopard 1 at Mailly that summer. According to Monsieur Roger Dannacker, there was little to differentiate between the Leopard and AMX-30 during these trials. [MP Robinson with thanks to Monsieur Roger Dannacker]

Production of the ARL-44 served more as a test of the government's ability to direct a weapons program.

As could have been expected, the experience of building the ARL-44 showed up very serious deficiencies in the French defence industry's ability to produce all the necessary components for a complex weapon system like a medium tank. The French government, in order to centralise control over the state arsenals tasked with domestic armoured vehicle production established the *Direction des Etudes et Fabrication d'Armament* (known by the acronym DEFA). DEFA served as a bureau tasked to direct

Place de la Concorde, 1976. A display of military equipment, including the AMX-13 SS-11 and AMX-30B. Here we can see the *Lodi* an AMX-30B of the 4e *Escadron*, 501e RCC. [Marcel Toulon]

A manual extract showing one of the préserie tanks. The PH-8A infrared searchlight was mounted to the left of the main armament. The layout of the glacis plate and the location for the battery cover plates (which covered the battery compartment vents during deep fording and river crossing operations) is not that seen on production tanks. The location of the turret radio aerial base is another give away. Given the fact this vehicle has the TOP-7 cupola fitted it is possibly the last definition vehicle. [Thomas Seignon]

Here is an early production vehicle depicted in another technical manual extract. The infrared searchlight is the PH-8B seen on production tanks. The glacis plate stowage layout is that standardized on the production tanks, and the aerial base has been moved to its definitive location. The main armament is at maximum elevation (+ 20°). The co-axial 12.7mm machine gun armament could be elevated separately to a higher angle (+40°). [Thomas Seignon]

army weapons procurement, design and production as a logical step forward from the ARL-44 program.

DEFA's first large ground-up project was the AMX-50 M4. The new design started off under the direction of *Ingenieur-Général* Joseph Molinié. Like the ARL-44, the AMX-50 M4 was intended to be a medium tank on the grand scale of the wartime *Panzerkampfwagen V* Panther. The project's design work was conducted by the *Atelier de Construction d'Issy-les-Moulineaux* (the state arsenal known commonly by the abbreviation of AMX). The resulting 45 to 50 ton designs were projected for construction by the *Atelier de Roanne*, and design work was commenced no sooner than the ARL-44 project went into production. Perhaps as a hedge because of the ARL-44's serious problems under government direction, the private firm of SOMUA was tasked by the army with designing a heavy tank to the same specification as the AMX-50 (which was designated SOMUA SM).

The oscillating turret designs employed on the 50 ton project resembled scaled-up versions of the FL10 and FL11 designs used on the AMX-13 light tank and EBR armoured car with automatic loading. The SOMUA project was dropped as a du-

plication of effort once the AMX-50 prototypes were deemed sufficiently satisfactory in 1954. With prototypes eventually ranging from 50 to 62 tons, the AMX-50 quickly exceeded the designed weight limit of 45 tons. The AMX-50's power train was a separately sourced sub-system, because DEFA did not control any automotive organizations and was devised with the intention to cooperate with France's existing automotive companies. Since France did not have a large enough engine in domestic production for a modern medium tank, the German wartime Maybach HL295 series of engines from the German Panther and Tiger tanks was selected to power the prototypes and would have served as the basis for the production engine.

The five AMX-50 prototypes all differed in detail and were repeatedly upgraded. On the AMX-50 M4 prototypes the main armament grew from the Schneider 90mm gun, to an *Atelier de Tarbes* 100mm piece. The prototypes also differed in the turret and hull configurations tried out on each vehicle. The use of overlapping wheels in the suspension and Panther tracks ensured that the AMX-50 hull appeared decidedly Teutonic, while the oscillating turret design gave all the AMX-50 prototypes a futuristic look. In terms of gunnery the design was expected

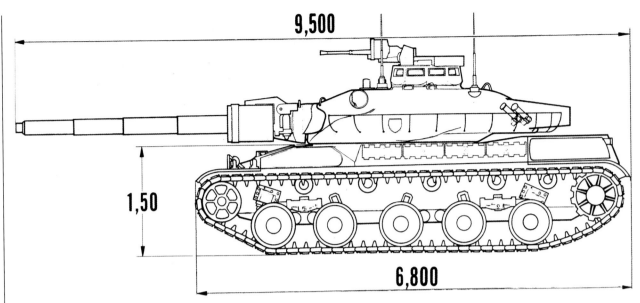

FIGURE 1
Cotes d'encombrement du char A.M.X. 30
(vue de profil)

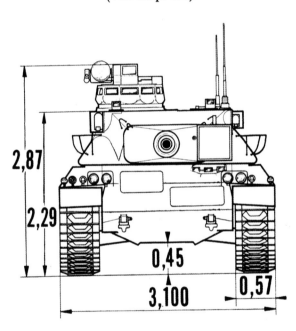

FIGURE 2
Cotes d'encombrement du char A.M.X. 30
(vue de face)

Basic dimensions of the AMX-30B, although the infrared searchlight is the PH-8A. The AMX-30 was quite a compact battle tank compared to its contemporaries. The adoption of the TOP7 resulted in a taller vehicle than Soviet tanks like the T62, but the AMX-30 had far better ergonomics. [Thomas Seignon]

to be able to engage targets rapidly due to its automatic loading system and at long range due to its use of an optical rangefinder.

The AMX-50 deliberately drew on German engineering where French component designs were still lacking and the design avoided American content. The first AMX prototype was ready in 1949 armed with a 90mm Schneider cannon in an oscillating turret at 53 tons, a commendable achievement for France's recovering industrial complex. It was refitted with *Atelier de Tarbes*' 100mm gun a few months later and was joined

by a second prototype. Bearing in mind that at this point the ARL-44 was only just entering service, the AMX-50 project had already achieved a strong result by producing two prototypes so quickly. The two AMX-50 prototypes actually participated in the 1950 Bastille Day parade, a moment symbolic for a nation that had been in ruins a mere five years before.

The possibility of rearming the West German army with French-built armoured fighting vehicles was a second impetus for getting the AMX-50 into production. This was an impossibly

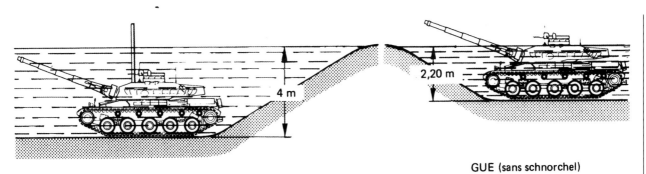

GUE (sans schnorchel)

GUE (avec schnorchel)

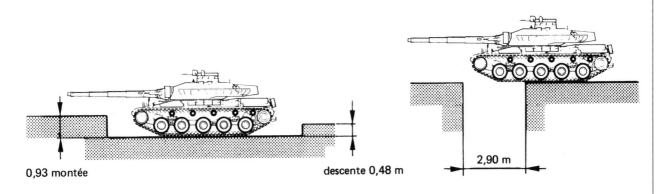

0,93 montée

descente 0,48 m

2,90 m

OBSTACLE VERTICAL

TRANCHEE (à bords francs)

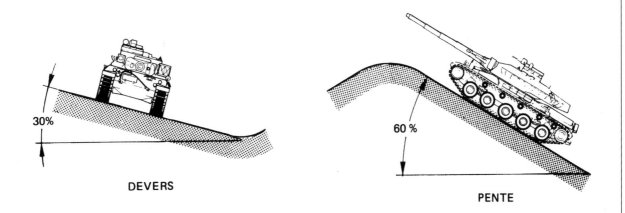

30%

60 %

DEVERS

PENTE

The basic mobility characteristics of the AMX-30. Naturally these figures were subject to weather and terrain. [Thomas Seignon]

tall order due to the other conflicting funding priorities France then was faced with, which included the war in Indo-China. It was obvious that production of the AMX-50 would require the economic support of the United States. There was already a fatal flaw in the AMX-50 design in 1950, more as a result of the state of France's heavy vehicle industry than as a result of poor tank design.

The basic weakness of the AMX-50 design was that it was powered by Maybach engines derived from those used in the wartime Panther and Tiger. These engines had been hard pressed to deliver enough power reliably in 1944, and still lacked sufficient power to deal with any increases in vehicle weight. The spin-on effect of the Maybach engine left the AMX-50 less well armoured than contemporary tanks of its size. It also meant that the powertrain was overtaxed and the level of reliability required could not be reached, despite repeated attempts to redesign the engine and transmission components. The hoped-for interest from other European Union armies did not materialise because

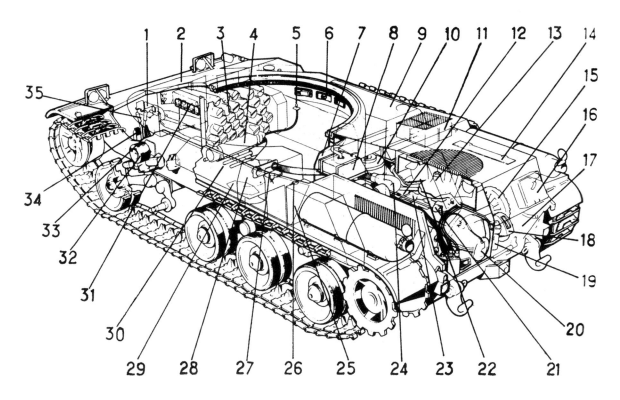

1. Gear Selector
2. Front Fuel Tank
3. 105mm Ammunition Magazine
4. CO2 bottle for fire suppression system
5. Fire suppression system activation switch (gunner's)
6. Fire detection alarm panel
7. Fire wall
8. Oil tank
9. Right rear fuel tank
10. Cooling pump
11. Batteries
12. HS110 engine
13. Main fan
14. Right radiator
15. Brake
16. Infantry telephone
17. Hinged lower hull plate
18. Steering brakes
19. Transmission filter
20. Transmission
21. Odometer wheel
22. Cooling system
23. Gearbox
24. Left side turbo compressor air intake
25. Left rear fuel tanks
26. Turret relief valve
27. Rotary junction
28. Air filter
29. Hatch
30. Torsion bars
31. Dashboard
32. Support roller
33. Accelerator pedal
34. Brake pedal
35. Steering levers

The AMX-30B hull layout can be seen from this exploded view. [Thomas Seignon]

of the long delays getting the design to a stage where production was a realistic option, and also due to the growing cost per unit of the vehicle. Ultimately American M47s were provided as military aid to France, West Germany, Belgium and Italy as a short term solution to rearmament needs. The offer of the M47 was too good for France to refuse in 1952, and the AMX-50 specification was changed from a medium to a heavy tank.

After the adoption of the Patton, the AMX-50 *Surblindé* project was re-specified as a heavy tank vehicle of some 60 tons, armed with a French built version of the 120mm American T53 gun made by the Atelier du Havre. Heavy tanks were not built in large production runs and the likelihood of exporting such a vehicle was slim. The changes in specification caused other delays and indicated that the basic concept behind the specification had to be re-evaluated at the general staff level. The AMX-50 program began to founder when the vehicle's end use was redefined into a class of vehicle that many considered a luxury (and especiallyfor an army still fighting in the colonies). As the cost of French military commitments in the colonies escalated, the utility of limited production, specialist weapons programs like heavy tanks began to cause doubts in the general staff. The last three AMX-50 prototypes got progressively heavier, which drove up unit costs and reduced the vehicle's horsepower per

ton ratio and engine reliability. As a matter of national pride, the AMX-50 program continued into 1956 regardless of these difficulties, with Maybach engineers brought in from Germany to solve the powertrain issues. By 1955-56 the lightened AMX-50 *Surbaissé* design was sufficiently well developed for production, but a tentative order for 100 vehicles for 1956 was delayed because the power output problems with the Maybach engine were as yet unresolved. Second thoughts arose during the delay, and the French Army was left to ponder the tactical implications of the heavy and costly AMX-50 in light of guided antitank missile development, and competing priorities such as the nuclear weapons program.

The funding arrangements that the French hoped the United States Military Aid Program would provide were never secured. The successful development of French light armoured tactics based on the AMX-13, guided missiles like the SS-11 then under development, and the availability of M47 Medium tanks weighed heavily against the AMX-50 program. The French Army re-examined the need for a heavy tank, and the AMX-50 program was suspended at the end of 1956, although the vehicles continued to be tested and modified until 1958. By 1955 the first of over eight hundred M47 Patton tanks had been delivered to the French Army as military aid from the United States. The

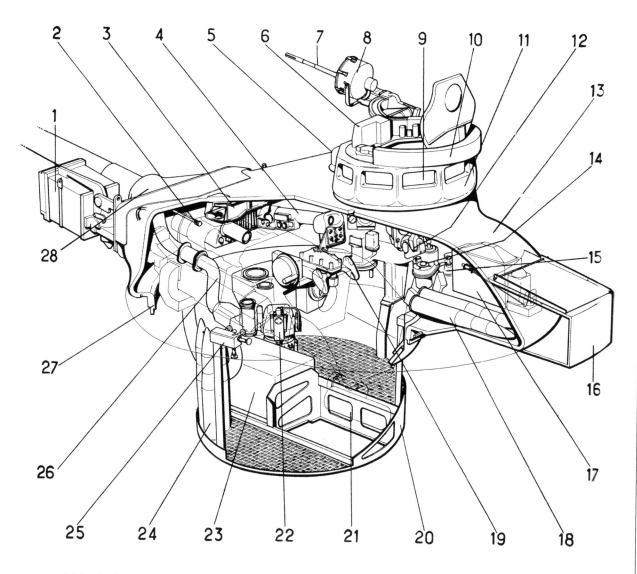

1. Infrared projector/ white light searchlight (Note the type shown is a PH-8A, the PH-8B was the correct type for a production vehicle)
2. Chamber evacuator control
3. M208 coincidence rangefinder
4. M271 main gunnery sight
5. Gunner's periscope mount (M282 day sight or OB17A infrared sight)
6. Commander's binocular sight mount (M267 day sight or OB23A infrared sight)
7. AAN 7.62mm cupola mounted machine gun
8. Cupola infrared projector/white light searchlight
9. M268 episcope
10. Cupola machine gun circular ammunition box
11. TOP7 cupola
12. Commander's position
13. Turret casting
14. Contra-rotation control box
15. Turret Lock
16. Turret bustle stowage bin
17. NBC filtration system
18. Turret bustle ammunition stowage
19. Gunner's position
20. Turret basket
21. Chamber fume evacuation system compressed air bottle
22. Turret traverse hydraulic motor
23. Radio mounting
24. 105mm ammunition 3 round ready rack
25. Compressed air control valve
26. Main armament chamber fume evacuation system
27. Turret race
28. Mantlet

A diagram showing the interior layout of the AMX-30B. Here again the PH-8A searchlight is shown, which is incorrect for a production vehicle (this diagram was included in several editions of the basic AMX-30 manual despite this fact!). The TOP-7 cupola offered a panoramic 360° view that was particularly valued by tank commanders, allowing them to work *head-in*. In battle this would have minimized the need to operate *head out*. [Thomas Seignon]

arrival of the Patton proved to be the fatal blow to the AMX-50, whose future as a design would surely have been brighter had it not been so often delayed and had funding been available.

French tactical priorities shifted towards the ideal of an armoured force operating within all-arms divisions. The army wanted a formation capable of strategic maneuver warfare in Europe or counter-insurgency in the colonies. The Indochina and Algerian campaigns had changed how the army prioritised its funding for weapons production. The dual role the army had to fill in the colonies and NATO meant that the equipment required for the armoured regiments emphasized firepower and mobility. The organizations used for infantry and armoured formations deployed in colonial warfare and in West Germany had to be interchangeable. The colonial battlefields demanded relatively simple and light armoured vehicles, while the European battlefield demanded all the latest technology to deal with potential enemy threats. The value of hollow charge warheads, rocket and guided missile technology, airborne forces and the battlefield helicopter all changed how France's strategists expected to configure their future armoured forces. With the failure of the AMX-50, the requirement for France's medium, or battle tank was re-evaluated with new eyes.

Projecteur
PH-8-B
volets ouverts

This image is from the PH-8B manual, which was opened and closed from inside the turret. It could be used without the infrared filter, in which case the platoon drill for night engagements was for two tanks to illuminate and two to fire, but the duration of illumination could not exceed 10 seconds. [Thomas Seignon]

The 30-ton Tank

The France was left with the very successful AMX-13 light tank design and the somewhat unsatisfactory M47 medium tank as the basis for its armoured force for the end of the 1950s. At

Lampe à incandescence
24 V - 250 W

Glace d'étanchéité

Fig. 3 - Projecteur volets ouverts - Filtre

The PH-8B infrared projector. The PH-8 could be used as a white light searchlight as well as an infrared gunnery searchlight. While this equipment was surpassed by passive and thermal viewing devices in the late 1970s, it remained part of the AMX-30B and AMX-30B2's equipment right into the 21st Century. In the infrared mode the PH-8B was effective to a range of 800-1000 meters but was easily detectable. In white light mode the searchlight could be used to illuminate targets 500 meters away. [Thomas Seignon]

the turn of the decade even the funding of a sufficient annual production of the AMX-13 was always a problem amongst many competing priorities, so the armoured force continued to include a number of wartime M4 and M24 tanks for secondary tasks and for colonial garrisons. The AMX-13 proved a very successful

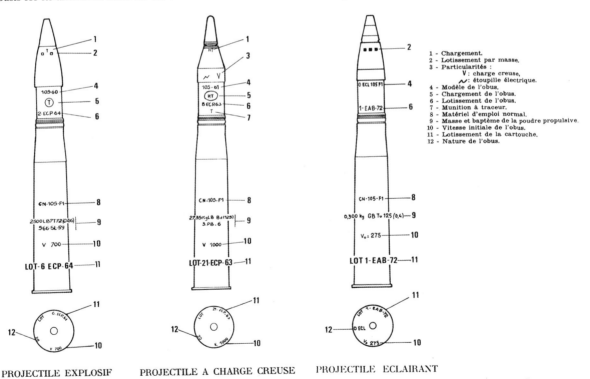

1 - Chargement.
2 - Lotissement par masse.
3 - Particularités :
   V : charge creuse,
   ～ : étoupille électrique.
4 - Modèle de l'obus.
5 - Chargement de l'obus.
6 - Lotissement de l'obus.
7 - Munition à traceur.
8 - Matériel d'emploi normal.
9 - Masse et baptême de la poudre propulsive.
10 - Vitesse initiale de l'obus.
11 - Lotissement de la cartouche.
12 - Nature de l'obus.

PROJECTILE EXPLOSIF   PROJECTILE A CHARGE CREUSE   PROJECTILE ECLAIRANT

Three of the main ammunition types used in the AMX-30B's CN 105 F-1, a powerful 105mm weapon still much respected in the French Army to the present day. These munitions were known as the 105 OE (high-explosive round), the 105 OCC (the famous hollow-charge HEAT round known as the Obus-G, whose rotation once fired was limited by an internal ball bearing race) and the 105 ÉCLAIR, an illuminating round that incorporated a parachute. Other munitions developed for the F-1 gun included a blank round, a smoke round, and naturally, in the early 1980s, a discarding sabot round known as the OFL (Obus Flèche) was adopted. [Thomas Seignon]

export within NATO and elsewhere (and achieved export sales second only to the Renault FT-17 in as a French tank design, to give some historical perspective). It carried the same punch as the wartime Panther in a 14-ton tank with a crew of three men.

Light mechanised divisions were evaluated as the best way to use the powerful light tank and its derivatives. An up-gunned version of the AMX-13 was briefly considered as a candidate for the *Char de Bataille*. The idea of such a light vehicle becoming the basis of the future *Char de Bataille* was rejected on the grounds that it was too small to carry enough ammunition, was not amphibious, and was not easily sealed against nuclear contamination. The M47 Patton was never seen as ideal as a weapon to arm France's armoured formations either, being considered too heavy and lacking the kind of fire power necessary to take on future Soviet tank designs.

The balance of qualities that the AMX-13 offered in the 1950s (firepower and mobility in a very light vehicle) was considered tactically sound in the French armoured corps. It coincided with a rebirth of the cavalry concepts of former times in French armoured tactical doctrine. This process started even while the AMX-50 program was being refined and was evident in the high power to weight ratio demanded in the AMX-50 specification. A light armoured formation was studied on an experimental basis in 1955, known as the *javelot* or javelin division. It was an all-arms division with the primary mission to fulfill France's conventional NATO commitments. A second purpose for a lighter and partly wheeled force employing the same organization but with older equipment could be found on counter-insurgency duties in Algeria. For NATO duties a great deal of the formation's firepower was expected to come from lightly armoured weapon systems like the AMX-13 family, and the division would be protected from heavy armour threats by antitank guided missile systems. The relative lack of staying power such a division might have in prolonged engagements against conventional enemy forces supported by heavy AFVs was accepted. At the time it was not a consideration that could be immediately addressed economically by the French army.

The French army of the day, still smarting from withdrawal from Indo China, was willing to adopt new tactics, but had to be very mindful of the need to balance low intensity warfare capabilities and NATO commitments within the national budget. The 1955 pattern *Division Mécanisée Rapide* (or DMR), was the French army's answer and was a result of much careful consideration. The DMR relied on technology and speed to win on the battlefield, in a complete change from the very backward tactics France had relied on in 1940, or even the U.S.-inspired combat teams that the Free French armoured divisions had employed in 1944.

The DMR was less expensive than a conventional armoured division. The theory for its use focused on inter-arms cooperation within large regiments, and it offered scope for future development as technology permitted. On the European battlefield it had to be mobile and equipped lightly enough to be able to disperse to avoid nuclear attack and then to reassemble swiftly to counterattack any Warsaw Pact thrust. The light weapon systems it employed were well thought out and modern and the doctrine for using the DMR suited its equipment. Logical outgrowths of the DMR incorporated self-propelled artillery and helicopter support, and in its NATO environment it intended to employ armoured infantry.

The organization of the *javelot* division theoretically allowed interchangeability of formations from West Germany to Algeria. The military and economic implications of such a fundamentally different divisional concept seemed promising in the mid-1950s and they deeply influenced French tactical thinking at all levels. Be it for reasons of cost, or because of the apparent success

105mm F-1 rounds laid out on plywood sheets during a range period. [C. Legrand]

105mm F1 rounds in their transport crates. Each wooden crate held two rounds in fiberboard tubes. [C. Legrand]

January 1978 on the FFA ranges with the *1e Régiment de Cuirassiers.* [Paul Baron]

AMX-30Bs of the 1ᵉʳ Régiment de Chasseurs d'Afrique (RCA) on the ranges at Canjuers in southern France. The tanks of the 1ᵉʳ RCA were put at the disposition of the ABC for range firing by crews from regiments from across the French armoured corps. Here we see range firing by individual tank crews. Tanks A,C and D have their guns at maximum elevation (+ 20°) while tank B conducts its firing. The red pennant on tank B indicates it has weapons loaded and ready, while the other three carry green pennants indicating that their weapons are clear. [Thomas Seignon]

Preparing a squadron firing exercise behind range CT35 at the Baumholder training area in Germany some time in 1991. We can see 12 of 17 AMX-30B tanks of the *4ᵉ Escadron* of the *6ᵉ Régiment de Dragons* . At this time the squadron organization was 4 platoons of 4 tanks each plus the captain's command tank (distinguished by its 3 antenna masts). [Thomas Seignon]

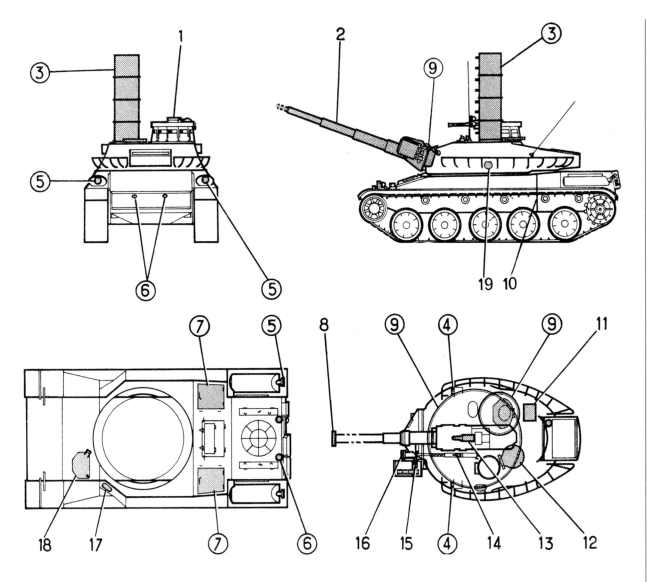

Deep Submersion Precautions (over 2 meter depth), AMX-30 Series:

1. Commander's hatch closed and locked
2. Gun at maximum elevation
3. Training tower in place and anchored (or combat schnorkel fitted)
4. Gun sight and rangefinder covers closed (AMX-30B)
5. Exhaust pipe hinged covers closed
6. Air intakes closed on rear plate
7. Battery compartment covers in place
8. Muzzle cover on main armament
9. Joint seals inflated
10. Fire wall vent open
11. NBC intake vent closed
12. Loader's hatch open (if using training tower only, otherwise loader's hatch closed and locked)
13. Main armament loaded
14. Co-axial armament loaded
15. Chamber fume evacuation valve closed
16. Obturator fitted to co-axial machine gun port or muzzle cover fitted to co-axial cannon
17. Crew heating air intake closed
18. Driver's hatch closed and locked
19. Shell loading/ejection port closed and locked

The basics of deep fording, and river crossing operations deeper than 2 meters in the AMX-30. The training tower is fitted in the examples described. Deep fording required substantial training and support, and was a daunting operation to some conscripts, especially those who had never learnt to swim. [Thomas Seignon]

of lighter tank designs under the new armoured doctrine, the French army was being firmly pushed towards a light medium tank design for its next battle tank program.

The ideal medium tank, at least as far as the general staff and DEFA envisioned, should weigh around 30 tons, carry a 105mm gun, and should depend on its very mobility for much of its protection. The *Char de Batignolles-Châtillon* prototype,

resembling an enlarged AMX13 at 25 tons, proved that the concept was within the possible, appearing in 1954 as a private venture from the Batignolles-Châtillon company of Nantes. This proposal was dismissed despite some useful design innovations, much like the earlier 40-ton *Char Lorraine 40T* medium tank design of 1952 (a sort of lightened version of the AMX-50 with a pneumatic tired suspension).

Belgique, turret number 443, of the *501e RCC* begins a submerged crossing with a training tower fitted to the loader's hatch in 1977. Note how the support lines for the tower are securely fixed to the turret and mantlet. [C. Legrand]

As an aside, the DMR concept, so promising in an army recovering from the shock of defeat in Indo-China, was also rejected in time. As in any peace time army, the different arms of service ended up competing for a leading role, and the *javelot* division quickly fell victim after its brief moment of glory at Suez. While the ideal of cavalry-inspired tactics of fighting reconnaissance and deep thrusts persisted well into the modern era (as standard doctrine), the large inter-arms regiments that the DMR was based on never took hold. The basic concept of the armoured division reincarnated in the Napoleonic spirit of a light cavalry formation persisted long after the *javelot* experiment ended, and it remains a strong ethos in the French armoured force to this day.

This 1979 photo shows an AMX30B *Valmy* of the *4e Regiment de Cuirassiers* entering the water during a submerged crossing at Lac Haspelschieltd, in 1979. It is fitted with the narrow combat schnorkel. [C. Balmefrezol]

These AMX-30Bs pausing on exercise in the 1970s are probably from the 503eRCC. [Jacques Maillard]

In the early 1960s the French *régiment de chars* stood as a four *escadron* (squadron) formation. Three squadrons held M47 Medium Tanks, the fourth had AMX-13 SS11 light tanks with 75mm guns and SS11 guided missiles, assuring an adequate antitank capability. Each *escadron* consisted of three *pelotons* (platoons) of five tanks each with a fourth platoon of infantry carried in three AMX-13 VTT armoured personnel carriers and two more AMX-13 VTT command vehicles in the command platoon. The idea of including organic infantry in the tank squadron and of including a tank company in each mechanised infantry regiment was the biggest part of the *javelot* spirit that could be salvaged at the regimental level. Beyond this, the army's more conservative elements and France's improving economy ensured that conventional armoured divisions would be the basis of the nation's NATO commitment.

The Europa Panzer

A coincidence to the shift in tactics towards a light medium tank design in France in the mid-1950s was paralleled in France's relationships within NATO. The FINBEL army general staff liaison group within the European Union agreed with the French vision of what design parameters a future European medium tank should adopt (FINBEL consisted of staff delegations from the armies of France, Italy, Netherlands, Belgium, and Luxembourg, and became FINABEL when West Germany joined in 1956). This group, which functioned outside of NATO, was organised to achieve some degree of consultative independence in military matters for the continental European NATO members, separate from the American-dominated NATO general staff conferences.

The French Army's suggested specification for a 30-ton medium tank was endorsed by the FINABEL representatives of the new West German *Bundeswehr*. West German rearmament was authorised in 1956 to expand into an army representative of West Germany's emerging role as a full NATO partner. The basic battle tank specification agreed upon in 1956 received the designation of FINABEL 3A5. Known by the rather more familiar name of the *Europa Panzer*, this multi-national specification was unique for its time. No equivalent was seen in the contem-

The PAFF divers standing on the EBR based escape training rig, training complete. PAFF divers were highly trained (including parachute qualification in many cases) and were selected from the *Genie*, or corps of engineers. [C. Legrand]

Satory 1985: Waiting their turn to cross the caisson, tanks and crews of the *501e RCC* inspect their vehicles. To the left, the tank already has a training tower fitted, while to the right we can see the training tower resting on the engine deck of 294 0105, the 105th AMX-30B built. Both of these tanks carry the 20mm secondary armament, retrofitted in the case of 294 0105, probably in the 1979-1980 period. [C. Legrand]

porary staff talks known as the Tripartite Conferences, which were held annually between the British, Canadian and American army general staffs. Heavier designs in the 40 to 45 ton class were envisioned and extensively discussed (the American T-95 and British Medium Gun Tank No.2) in the Anglo-American tank programs at around the same time.

Within the FINABEL group there was strong sentiment against having to accept American weaponry for the future armament of the continental European NATO armies. Much as it had hoped to sell the AMX-50 a few years earlier, France in particular hoped to turn the need for a 30-ton tank to the advantage of its armaments industry. Paradoxically, all the FI-

Satory 1985: with an AMX-30D waiting in case of breakdown and the PAFF zodiac visible on the left, an AMX-30B crosses with training tower fitted. [C. Legrand]

This is possibly 294 0105 climbing out of the caisson. Crossings required solid radio communications and were a very unique experience for the men involved. [C. Legrand]

EXTEL Demeter in October 1988 included deep fording as can be seen, the combat schnorkel being fitted on this tank's loader's hatch, just as it would be in the case of an actual combat river crossing. [C. Legrand]

NABEL members by 1956 were re-equipping with American or American funded British equipment as their basic means of rearmament.

The FINABEL 3A5 specification evolved further from staff talks between the French, West German and Italian armies that followed in 1956-57, which agreed on substantial weapon standardization and co-production. It was a brilliant ideal to have the bulk of NATO's largest continental European armies equipped with common weapon systems. At this time the

West German *Bundeswehr* was being equipped with the M47 Medium Tank, as were France and Italy. A bilateral agreement was signed by France and Germany on the 27th of October 1956, joined by Italy in May 1957. The three nations' general staffs had a common requirement for a highly mobile main battle tank in the coming decade.

The three armies agreed on a 30-ton tank armed with a 105mm gun as the basic design requirement, with agreements for complete design projects to be conducted in both

La Marne, fitted with a training tower over the loader's position, starts a submerged crossing. [Thomas Seignon]

West Germany and France being signed on 28th of November 1957. Italy was incapable of tank production at the time. All three armies agreed to evaluate the completed prototypes and to select a standard vehicle, which would then be adopted as the standard battle tank in the three armies. The Europa Panzer could hopefully then be produced for the armies of the other FINABEL members.

Despite a rapid advance towards the design of prototypes, in 1958 the first signs of divergence within the Franco-German partnership appeared. Charles de Gaulle, starting as the prime minister and defence minister in June 1958, was in favour of a rapprochement with West Germany but was opposed to many of the bilateral agreements that had up to then been drafted between the two countries. His position included opposition to several of the strategic and economic issues already outlined and agreed upon in the 1951 Treaty of Paris. He also vetoed sharing nuclear weapon technology with West Germany, a concession agreed to in the Colomb-Béchar protocol of June 1957. His position was based on the premise that France was a great power and required to keep its independence in all strategic matters whatever its alliances. To the Germans it seemed that the French leader was unwilling to conduct an alliance with the Germans as equal partners. The West Germans were incensed at what was seen by many Germans as a French denial to them of the strongest deterrent against possible Soviet aggression. The West German defence minister refused to accept the role

of junior partner in his country's dealings with France, and naturally turned to the Americans for support.

The West German defence minister henceforth opposed French leadership in existing agreements wherever he could (and his confidence grew quickly, as arms production capability arose as a part of West Germany's already impressive economic recovery in 1960). The detail points of the Europa Panzer's design philosophy seemed as good a place as any to oppose French nationalism, and the previously positive partnership within the project quickly soured. Work on the prototypes in France and Germany began in the spirit of competition, not cooperation.

The method that the Germans employed to allow a speedy development of their tank design relied on government managed competition between two syndicates of private heavy engineering companies. It stood in stark contrast to the DEFA-dominated development path of the *Char de Bataille*, which was almost completely managed through one state-run bureau and the arsenals it controlled. The French 30 ton prototypes were designed by the *Atelier de Construction d'Issy les Moulineaux* (AMX) engineering team under the direction of Joseph Molinié and was designated AMX-30. Drawing on the experience accrued from the AMX 50-ton and 13-ton tank projects and from the testing of the *Char de Batignolles-Chatillon* prototype, the parameters for the new vehicle were already well known. These included a conventional turret with a 105mm main armament, a departure from the oscillating turrets of the previous

A bizarre looking adaption of an EBR Chassis, designed to train AMX-30 crews in underwater evacuation in the case of an underwater breakdown. The interior compartment was set up to permit the crew to practice evacuation through the tank's fighting compartment and out the driver's hatch. The essentials of the drill included the use of personal oxygen bottles, and each crew member had to wait their turn, exiting via the driver's hatch. The EBR chassis was progressively drowned in a 4 meter deep basin, the drill was conducted and the crew members were then rescued by the waiting PAFF team. The ultimate test was performing the drill in total darkness at night. [Thomas Seignon]

The *4e Régiment de Cuirassiers*, based at Bitche in eastern France, a unit often photographed training at the Lac Hapselschieldt. Here we see an AMX-30B charging out of the water with the training tower fitted in 1978. [P. Besson]

two AMX tank designs. The gun selected was the CN 105 F-1, a 105mm piece designed to fire hollow charge ammunition developed with German participation at the *Institut Saint Louis* (the *Obus Gessner* or *Obus-G*).

This HEAT round was unique in that it suspended the hollow charge shell on an internal bearing race to reduce the round's spin, which prevented degradation of the hollow charge's effect (a persistent problem faced by previous attempts to fire hollow charge munitions through rifled guns). As a result the F-1 gun's rifling twist was less severe than similar guns designed to fire kinetic energy rounds. The F-1 gun had a range of up to 3000 metres firing the *Obus-G* (or more officially the *Obus*

Tank 111 of the *4e Régiment de Cuirassiers* enters the water in 1978. [P. Besson]

Exiting the water, a moment that probably brought on a sigh of relief from the crew! This is probably tank 101 of the *4e Régiment de Cuirassiers*. [P. Besson]

A closeup of the AMX-30B in the water with the training tower fitted. We can see the tank has not yet reached the lowest point of the bottom of the Lac Hapschieldt. This tank was from the *4e Régiment de Cuirassiers* and was photographed in 1978. [P. Besson]

Charge Creuse 105mm F-1, usually abbreviated to OCC 105 F1). The early estimates for the hollow charge round's armour penetration characteristics were given as 350-400 mm of homogenous steel, which the design team at AMX confidently imagined would dispel the need for a kinetic energy armour piercing round. The main advantage from the use of hollow charge rounds was the long engagement range that could be expected, as a result of the chemical energy attack such a round relied on for its effectiveness. The penetration possible with the *Obus G* was consistent regardless of range, which arguably made the CN 105 F-1 gun in 1960 a weapon with superior antitank qualities than the kinetic rounds fired by the L7 gun at long ranges. Long range engagements theoretically allowed the design to carry lighter armour, and less weight.

With good observation and with the commander's M208 coincidence range finder to match the F-1 gun, the AMX-30 was expected to conduct most of its engagements at long range. The SOFAM flat 12 cylinder petrol engine, already tested on one of the two *Char de Batignolles-Chatillon* medium tank prototypes would be employed. The new medium tank would rely on its

A closeup of the AMX-30B in the water with the training tower fitted. We can see the tank has reached the lowest point of the bottom of the Lac Hapschieldt. This tank was from the *4e Régiment de Cuirassiers* and was photographed in 1978. [P. Besson]

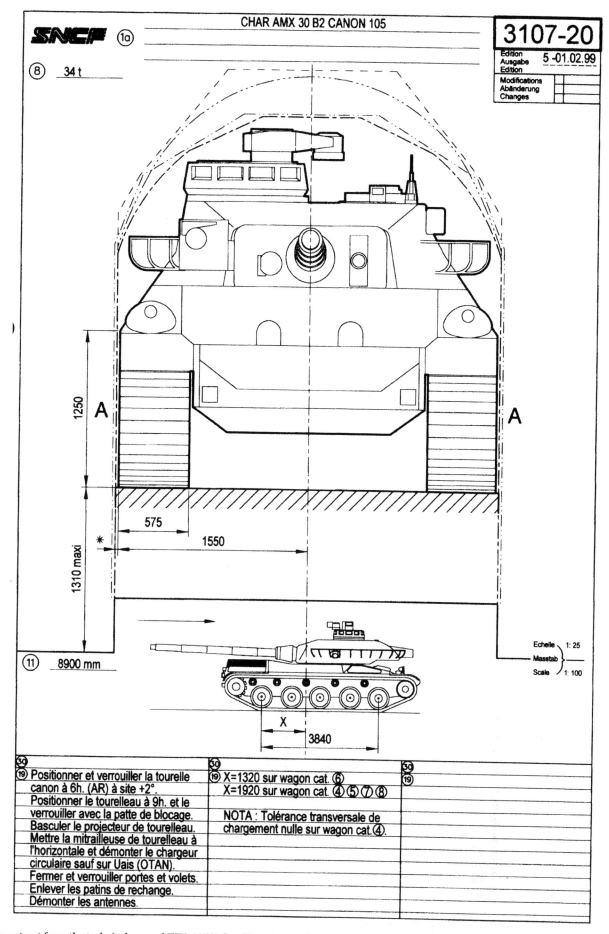

CHAR AMX 30 B2 CANON 105

3107-20

Edition Ausgabe Edition	5 -01.02.99
Modifications Abänderung Changes	

SNCF (1a)

(8) 34 t

1250

A

A

575

1550

1310 maxi

*

(11) 8900 mm

Echelle 1: 25
Masstab
Scale 1: 100

X

3840

(30)	(30)	(30)
(19) Positionner et verrouiller la tourelle canon à 6h. (AR) à site +2°. Positionner le tourelleau à 9h. et le verrouiller avec la patte de blocage. Basculer le projecteur de tourelleau. Mettre la mitrailleuse de tourelleau à l'horizontale et démonter le chargeur circulaire sauf sur Uais (OTAN). Fermer et verrouiller portes et volets. Enlever les patins de rechange. Démonter les antennes.	(19) X=1320 sur wagon cat. (6) X=1920 sur wagon cat. (4)(5)(7)(8) NOTA : Tolérance transversale de chargement nulle sur wagon cat.(4).	(19)

An extract from the technical manual TTA 126/2 detailing the requirements for rail travel (in this case for the AMX-30B2) on the SSys 50 ton wagon. We can see that clearances are very precise. This document could be found in the vehicle manual carried on board every tank. [Thomas Seignon]

The railway is an often used method of moving tank units, despite its higher cost compared to employing tank transporters. Here an escadron of the 1ᵉ RC is in course of embarking their AMX-30Bs at Trier station in West Germany. The first measures for rail travel have been taken: the TOP7 cupola is rotated to the 9 o'clock position, the cupola machinegun and ammunition feed box has been removed. The PH9 cupola searchlight has been pointed down, and of course all the vehicle antennae have been removed to avoid contact with overhead electrical lines! [Thomas Seignon]

Once on the wagon, the tank is secured and shackled with the turret in the 6 o'clock position. This SSys-50 ton wagon was designed in the 1940s for Tiger and Panther tanks by the Reichbahn, vehicles weighing some 20 and 7 tons more than an AMX-30B respectively. [Thomas Seignon]

speed and agility for protection, and the design was optimised to survive on a nuclear battlefield. The first AMX-30 prototype (as it was now known) was ready in September 1960. The AMX-30 prototype was a fine looking machine, exceptionally compact and agile, and if its armour was intentionally thin, it was well laid out and sloped.

The thin armour of the AMX-30 was the most controversial element of the design, and it was a design philosophy that was rejected by the United States, Great Britain, and eventually also by West Germany. It is easy enough to understand the position of the French design philosophy however. The armoured doctrine of the French army by the late 1950s was based on using lightly armoured, highly mobile and heavily armed vehicles. France also threw its lot in with the future success of anti-tank missile technology, a field its scientists then dominated. The doctrine the AMX design team believed in discredited the reliance on heavy protection in battle tank design, and the AMX-30 was a product of that doctrine.

A lighter battle tank was also cheaper to produce and procure in theory. This was an important consideration for a vehicle which *Direction Technique des Armements Terrestres* (or DTAT, as DEFA was renamed) hoped to sell to all of the FINABEL armies. Each nation in FINABEL was a welfare state with relatively small defence budget. Destined for a conscript army, the AMX-30 design was intentionally simple and was intended to allow quick training and mastery of its sub-systems. The potential of the vehicle as the Europa Panzer envisioned in 1957 was fast evaporating however. The unravelling of the

multinational basis of the design came as a result of France's continuing need to reassert itself as a great power. Largely because of France's nationalist foreign policies with regards to its NATO allies, which came to be known as *Gaullism*, German willingness to pursue the original ideal of the FINABEL 3A5 dwindled. Unfortunately for France's plans to dominate the NATO tank market with the AMX-30, the emergence of a strong West German industrial base coincided with the cooling of Franco-German relations.

De Gaulle's biggest step in assuring France's independence in strategic matters was to begin the process to remove French forces from NATO's formal military control. Despite remaining a member state of NATO this gave France the ability to opt out of certain NATO resolutions and to retain the ability to make its own military decisions without consulting its allies, which infuriated West Germany, Great Britain and the United States. Although this process was not formally completed until 1966, the move toward an independent foreign policy had begun as soon as De Gaulle took power as Prime Minister in 1958 and grew as De Gaulle's control over French foreign policy was extended. The objective of De Gaulle's policies ultimately came because of his failure to have the United States and the United Kingdom recognise France as an equal within NATO.

Gaullism was supposed to ensure that France could manage its own affairs without complete reliance on the United States. The penalty for its arms industry was that the French defence industry was rapidly isolated from arms markets that previous administrations had spent nearly ten years preparing to

Loading an AMX-30B onto an SSys wagon operated by the SNCF. The detachable loading ramp (known in the French Army as a QBD or *Quai en Bout Démontable*) could be used from the siding or directly on the rails and formed part of the standard equipment in each armoured regiment. The number 441 on the turret bustle bin identifies a tank of the *4e peloton* of the *4e escadron* of the 6e Régiment de Dragons. [Thomas Seignon]

As indicated by the NATO armoured regiment symbol on the front left mudguard of this AMX-30B, here is a vehicle of the *4ᵉ Escadron* of the *6ᵉ Régiment de Dragons* (RD). Like the 1ᵉ RC, the 6ᵉ RD was part of the 1ᵉ Division Blindée, stationed in the FFA in Germany. This photos was taken in 1991, by which time most AMX-30Bs had been fitted with the 20mm co-axial cannon. Guided by the vehicle commander, this tank has just climbed aboard a tank transporter. [Thomas Seignon]

Rhine ferries were operated by a specific unit of the French corps of engineers based in Strasbourg. Dated the 26th of May 1981, the AMX-30B on board is an early vehicle retrofitted with the 20mm F2 co-axial cannon. [Thomas Seignon]

Taken in the early 1970s, this photograph shows an inspection of the *1e Régiment de Cuirassiers*. Note the regimental insignia painted on the rangefinder "ears". [Paul Baron]

dominate. The *Bundeswehr* was rebuilt largely with American weaponry, and Germany was allowed after 1960 to resume heavy weapons manufacture. Within two years German firms were entering into direct competition with the companies and bureaus of the French defence industry. In the meantime the Germans had been driven directly into a closer arms procurement relationship with the United States and Great Britain by French policies.

The immediate effect on the AMX-30 project was that the United States pushed for the Royal Ordnance L-7 105mm gun to be adopted as the standard NATO tank gun. West Germany duly moved away from its own Rheinmetal the French 105mm gun and the *Obus-G* since the United States had developed an effective HEAT round for the British gun, which had been chosen to arm the M60 Main Battle Tank. West Germany accepted substantial quantities of American

An inspection in the 1970s at the *Quartier Welvert*, home base of the *1ᵉ Régiment de Cuirassiers* (or 1ᵉ RC) in West Germany. Individual weapons carried at the time for the tank crew were the MAT-49 SMG, with the exception of the tank commander, who was armed with a MAC-50 9mm pistol. In the background we can see the regimental commander's tank *Turenne*. The 1ᵉ RC emblem of the tower of Auvergne painted on the rangefinder ears was the heraldric emblem of the Maréchal de Turenne, first commander of the regiment. [Thomas Seignon]

The *Du Breuil*, an AMX-30B belonging to the *1e Escadron* of the *1er Régiment de Cuirassiers* based at St Wendel in the Rhineland-Palatinate area of West Germany in May 1973. This early production vehicle is not yet equipped with the wire mesh exhaust silencer covers. This photograph was taken on a Bundeswehr firing range near Koblenz, in the background we can see two Leopards belonging to the 3 Kompanie, Panzerabteilung 144. [Thomas Seignon]

The AMX-30B *Austerlitz*, the *1e Régiment de Cuirassiers'* second in command's mount (the commanders's tank was named *Turenne*). On the occasion captured in the photograph a lieutenant of the regiment is carrying the regimental standard during a command handover ceremony in West Germany in the 1970s. "Austerlitz", being a regimental battle honor emblazoned on the standards of many French cavalry regiments, was a very common name for the AMX-30s of squadron and regimental commanders in the ABC! [Thomas Seignon]

Maintaining track tension was part of the driver's job. Track adjustment was performed from the front end of the tank by adjusting the idler wheel position using a socket, 1.2 metre extension and ratchet. The AMX-30 series carried an extensive tool kit, never symbolic of a tank with an easy maintenance schedule. The driver, in this case from the 1er RC, does not look overly pleased with his task! [Thomas Seignon]

Maintenance inspection for tank 231. Maintenance was never the favourite task of a tank crew, but despite this fact (and the high proportion of conscripts in tank crews) the vehicle availability in armoured regiments was generally good. [Thomas Seignon]

weaponry (including the M113 carrier, M48 battle tank and M109 self-propelled howitzer) as a stopgap for its own weapon programs, a further snub to French ambitions to sell its relatively advanced military designs within NATO. France had already finalised the basic parameters of the AMX-30 by 1959 and West Germany began detail work on their own Leopard tank. The intent to adopt a common design by 1960 had thus completely disappeared.

France continued with the design of the AMX-30, with two prototypes running in September 1960 and July 1961. A second batch of seven *préserie* prototypes was built in 1962. Counting the final two pre-production series definition tanks, eleven

Moving along on one of the Champagne training grounds, a late production AMX-30B wears the 3 colour camouflage adopted by the French Army starting in 1984. The camouflage pattern was standardized and was applied the same on every vehicle. Although the general effect was similar to the NATO camouflage scheme worn by the Bundeswehr and United States Army, the colours employed were French standard colours and were not the same tones. The guard protecting the cupola machine gun is clearly visible, despite the fact that the machine gun itself is not fitted. [Thomas Seignon]

Photo taken in 1976 at the *501e RCC* base *Quartier Estienne* at Rambouillet. The AMX-30Ds were first issued in 1974 and until 1977-78 the old M74 recovery vehicles that had been loaned to France with the M47 Pattons were still on strength in some units. [C. Legrand]

prototypes were built. The first two vehicles weighed 32 tons and employed the powerful petrol powered SOFAM 12 GS ds 12-cylinder engine producing a remarkable 22 horsepower per ton. The weight grew to 36 tons by the time the design was judged fit for series production. The jump in tonnage was due to the decision to change engines. Much as in other contemporary NATO tank projects, the multi-fuel engine concept was adopted for the AMX-30 during the late 1950s. This led the design team to drop the SOFAM engine. The French chose to adopt the fairly conventional water-cooled diesel HS-110 design from the Hispano-Suiza division of the SNECMA organization, which would be produced under license by the Saviem division of Renault.

The new engine gave 680 horsepower and was of similar size to the SOFAM engine, though the output ratio dropped

somewhat to 20 horsepower per ton. While the transition from petrol to diesel engines resulted in some delay and was the closest to a multi-fuel requirement that the design ever came to accommodating. By 1963 eight AMX-30 vehicles, including at least one of the original two prototypes, had received the new HS-110 engines. The HS-110 diesel proved to be a somewhat troubled design in its early years (largely due to cooling issues), but it was the AMX-30's transmission that eclipsed it as a weak point of the design. The AMX-30B's transmission problems were recognised from the early stages of the program, but were never satisfactorily resolved before production began in 1966.

While it has long been understated in the case of the early Leopard and M60, none of the new generation of NATO MBTs were particularly reliable mechanically in the early stages of their development and service. In the case of the AMX-30 and the British Chieftain, it would take years before the desired level of reliability was reached in the early 1980s, and the publicity the mechanical issues received affected foreign sales. The rush into production despite the AMX-30B's feeble transmission came as a result of the need to use the available funding before priorities changed, and because of the financial desirability of selling the new tanks to other nations in order to defray the cost of developing such a complex weapon system. It was a gamble that did not succeed in securing large export orders.

Developments in West Germany had also proceeded at a rapid pace, with the *Standardpanzer* project split between two competing private sector groups, with the British L7 gun specified as main armament (a few of the prototypes mounted a Rheinmetall smoothbore 105mm gun to fire the Gessner round, but ultimately this option was dropped very early in the program). French efforts to sell the Germans the CN 105 F1 were unsuccessful despite the fact that the gun was rapidly proven to be an effective design. Of the two competing consortiums, the Porsche-led group developed a simple and cost effective hull design which quickly demonstrated a more favourable time to production stage. Both hull designs had mounted a common cast turret design with an optical rangefinder.

The West German method of managing competition between two conglomerates' designs seems to have been executed

Night maneuvers near Ronchamps in 1979. An AMX-30B, number 200 *Austerlitz* of the *2e Escadron, 6e Régiment de Dragons* is seen here experiencing mechanical difficulties. [C. Balmefrezol]

The tank commander, on the right side of the picture, hears the diagnosis. As was often the case, it is probably the transmission. Until the Minerva transmission was introduced on the AMX-30B2, the *Char de Bataille* suffered frequent transmission failures. This vehicle will likely wait for recovery until morning. [C. Balmefrezol]

A *Lieutenant* of the *6e Regiment de Dragons* photographed in 1979 wearing the first pattern of tank helmet issued to AMX-30 crews, the *Sous-Casque Radio Modèle 1965*, worn well into the 1980s and with an outer shell of hard plastic. Though it was almost never used as such, it was designed to fit under the *Modèle 1951* steel helmet. [C. Balmefrezol]

particularly well. It allowed a fast development process, a wider experience of actual production and the selection of a sound powertrain. The West Germans also had designs on selling most of the continental European NATO members their Leopard. Despite the fact that it was now a mere formality, the agreed upon trilateral evaluation of the French and West German tanks still had to be observed.

By 1962 some twenty six pre-production Leopard tanks were delivered to *Panzerlehrabteilung 93* at Munster for troop trials. At the same time the AMX-30 project was less advanced, and the number of development vehicles produced was not half of that made available to the *Bundeswehr*. The following year between September and October 1963 the final comparative trials between five of the AMX-30 *préserie* vehicles and five Leopard tanks took place. Although from the perspective of the French army team little differentiated the vehicles in terms

The AMX-13 VTT was France's first postwar APC, serving alongside the M47 through the 1960s and subsequently until 1979 alongside the AMX-30B in French armoured regiments, providing an ideal mount for the men of the *escadron porté*. [C. Legrand]

The *501e RCC's Andelot*, fitted with an air recognition panel as a barrel sleeve for exercise identification and bogged down in the chalky mud of a stream bank at Mailly in 1981. [C. Legrand]

Another view of *Andelot*, which will require recovery to get itself out of the thick Champagne mud. [C. Legrand]

of performance, the defence press of the time seems to have backed the West German design. Not only did the Leopard perform to expectation at the trial, its L7 gun's versatility firing a variety of NATO standard ammunition arguably gave a better showing. The West German design showed better mechanical characteristics, better agility and acceleration.

Satisfied with their L56 F-1 105mm gun despite the certainty that NATO would standardize on the British gun, proposals to combine the West German hull design with the French turret were also examined by the French design team. The idea was something of a last ditch effort to keep the multinational spirit in the project or to salvage some opportunities for the French arsenals in the event of the French gun being adopted by some of the potential clients, but it failed to attract any commitments. Both France and West Germany adopted their own Europa Panzers and it was left to each country to attempt to sell as many as possible to defray the development costs. The first to market would logically secure orders.

The unravelling of France's efforts to sell the AMX-30 as the Europa Panzer

Whether the Leopard had demonstrated superior characteristics or whether *Gaullism* had poisoned the chances for the AMX-30's adoption by the FINABEL members, the AMX-30 was not yet ready for production because DTAT's arsenals still had to tool up. In 1963 the French government announced it would adopt the AMX-30B (B for Char de *Bataille*), ordering 300 vehicles, but would delay production until 1965 due to funding. In West Germany the Leopard was definitively ordered for the *Bundeswehr* at the end of 1963, with production of 1400 vehicles beginning as soon as possible. The large *Bundeswehr* order for the Leopard resulted in the selection of more than one production contractor and more than one assembly line. The AMX-30 production line at the *Atelier de Roanne*, for a variety of reasons but largely because of funding, began to build the

With another AMX-30B on the scene, an attempt begins by the crews of the two vehicles to pull *Andelot* free. We can surmise the exercise will not do the transmission of either tank much good! The crewmen begin to attach a towing hawser. [C. Legrand]

The rescuers gun their engine pulling *Andelot* free. Note the smoke from the HS110 diesel. An AMX-30D from the recovery platoon will not be required. [C. Legrand]

new tank in 1965 but did not reach full scale production capacity until 1971. For the first five production years (1966-1970) only 10 to 15 vehicles per month could be delivered.

The French Army's 1967 pattern *divisions mecanisées*, for which the new tanks were destined, were ready for their tanks long before the vehicles had all arrived. NATO orders for the AMX-30 did not materialise as hoped and the all the while the West Germans very successfully marketed their new Leopard. The Krauss-Maffei production line delivered its first production Leopard in September 1965. The Netherlands, who were also courted by the British to replace their Centurions with Chieftains, decided to supplement their Centurion fleet with Leopards instead. Belgium, who had evaluated both the AMX-30 and the Leopard, decided in favour of the West German design when the French refused to consider co-production or Belgian content. Italy accepted the offer of co-production of the M60

The turret crew return to *Andelot*, probably to resume their role in the exercise. Note the insignia of the 2e Division Blindée on the front slope of the turret wall. [C. Legrand]

With lights blazing, the AMX-30Bs and AMX-10Ps of the *501e Régiment de Chars de Combat* parade through Paris by night on the 14th of July 1982. From the early 1970s the 501e RCC was the unit most often tasked with high profile parades. By 1982 it already had a completely professionalised *2e Escadron*, from which the implications of a professionalised regiment were studied and perfected over the span of over a decade. [C. Legrand]

by the United States but later also ordered over 800 Leopards for her army, receiving a production license. The Leopard had won out over the AMX-30 as the Europa Panzer.

Exports

The AMX30B was in fact not ordered by any other foreign army until 1969, when Greece ordered 190 AMX-30B tank and 14 AMX-30D recovery vehicles. Spain ordered a small batch of 19 AMX-30B the following year. The sale of a production license to Spain for some 280 vehicles followed in 1972, with assembly to be undertaken at the *Empressa Nacional Santa Barbara* plant at Seville. The AMX-30E as it was known in Spain had a troubled history and by all accounts its adoption had more to do with the refusal of some NATO countries to sell arms to the Franco regime than with an outright preference for the AMX-30. Thus only Greece and Spain bought the AMX-30 out of the host of NATO nations, in numbers totalling some 600 battle tanks and support vehicles. This effectively had to be considered as a failure of one of France's major aims in the 30-ton tank program, although in the later part of the decade French sales strategies for the AMX-30B were more successful when the sale of AMX-30B tanks were arranged with Chile (20 tanks delivered), Venezuela (85 tanks delivered from an order for 142 placed in 1972), Saudi Arabia (190 tanks ordered), Qatar (54 tanks), United Arab Emirates (64 tanks ordered in 1977, later augmented with AMX-30B2 tanks and re-sold to Bosnia following the UAE's adoption of the Leclerc Main Battle Tank) and other smaller armies ensued as target markets outside of NATO were identified, often where the Leopard could not be sold for political reasons. The later AMX-30B2 was also sold to Cyprus (40 tanks later augmented with at least 60 ex-Greek AMX-30B tanks).

The AMX-30B: the *Char de Bataille* enters service

The French army's order was increased to over 900 AMX-30 series vehicles in 1965. Eventually these orders were increased again to include over 1100 AMX-30B gun tanks. The first unit to receive test vehicles had been formed under the *501e Régiment de Chars de Combat* based at Rambouillet, where a small testing ground existed to permit vehicle evaluation. After the

These AMX-30B tanks of the *501e RCC* are being bulled up for an inspection 1985. We can see the *Eylau* here amongst others. Note the crewmen in two types of service dress. The blue overalls are worn with the older pattern leather belt, the green combat uniform is worn with a canvas web belt. [C. Legrand]

The *mecanos* hard at work on the power train of an AMX-30B of the *501e RCC* during preparations for inspection in 1985. They will be hoisting the power pack out with the gantry if necessary. Note how the hull rear plate has already been removed. [C. Legrand]

The 501e RCC's tank park in November 1985. The third tank visible on the left is the *Lutzen*. [C. Legrand]

The snowy tank park at Mailly in the winter of 1985. [C. Legrand]

autumn 1963 trials against the Leopard under the trials unit led by *Capitaine* Gamache, these 7 vehicles (referred to at the time as AMX-30A) were used for further trials and to test components. They were transferred as crew trainers to the first regiment scheduled to train for full equipment with the production standard AMX-30B in 1966; the *503e Régiment de Chars de Combat* at Mourmelon.

The *503e Régiment de Chars de Combat* (or 503e RCC, which along with the 501e RCC was one of the two armoured regiments in the French Army that had survived as heirs of France's original tank regiments of the First World War) re-

An early AMX-30B, seen here with the co-axial .50 caliber machinegun fitted. The early batches of AMX-30B tanks were finished with the .50 caliber secondary armament, and although some tanks retained their original coaxial weapons until they were decommissioned at the end of the Cold War, most AMX-30Bs were fitted with the 20mm F2 cannon in the late 1970s and early 1980s. The PH-8B IR projector is not fitted to this tank. [F. Cany]

Here we can see the *Austerlitz* refuelling at Mailly in May 1986. *Austerlitz* was the squadron command tank of the *2e Escadron* of the *501eRCC*. The *501eRCC* was the only French unit that took the AMX-30B outside of its NATO deployment area in the FFA or metropolitan France, when it deployed the *2e Escadron* to Africa. [C. Legrand]

The Berliet GBC 8KT CCT tactical refuelling truck was used to fuel up to 4 AMX-30s at the same time. [Thomas Seignon]

The Berliet GBC 8KT CCT had excellent all terrain performance and was an essential part of the logistics platoon. [Thomas Seignon]

Photographed in 1986, two *2e Escadron* AMX-30B tanks of the *501e RCC* receive their daily maintenance checks at Mailly. Beginning in 1978, the *2e Escadron* of the *501eRCC* was professionalized and was for over a decade the only professionalised tank squadron in the entire ABC. The correct abbreviation in French Army terminology for the squadron would be *2/501e RCC*. [C. Legrand]

The *Austerlitz* is shown here being fuelled up by a crewman in May 1986. By this time some AMX-30 regiments of the FFA were beginning to implement the 3-tone NATO camouflage. Because the *501e RCC* was based in eastern France, it kept the overall *vert armée* paint scheme later than units based in Germany. By the mid-1990s the 3-tone NATO scheme (also adopted by the Bundeswehr, the Canadian Army, and most units of the United States Army) had replaced the single tone scheme entirely. [C. Legrand]

An AMX-30B of 2/501RCC in 1986 during *EXTEL Crevecoeur* in September 1987. Note the tactical symbol on the front left mudguard which shows the unit and formation (*escadron*, regiment, division) as well as the standard NATO symbol for an armoured regiment. This vehicle is carries the *numero d'immatriculation* 294 0091. The loader is conversing with a soldier in full infantry fighting order, probably from the *escadron's peleton porté*. [C. Legrand]

A break for crews of AMX30B tanks of the 2/501RCC during *EXTEL Crevecoeur*. Note how the tanks (factory painted in *vert armée* until the late 1980s) have been camouflaged with mud applied to a pattern of wide bands. The tanks carry fire simulator gear for the purpose of the exercise. [C. Legrand]

ceived the first production AMX-30B tanks in batches sufficient to re-equip a single squadron at a time, starting in at the end of 1966 at Mourmelon. By the time of the Bastille Day parade on July 14th 1967, two squadrons led by their *chef de corps, Colonel* Huberdeau, paraded their tanks down the *Champs Élysées* in Paris. Marching before De Gaulle himself with 26 tanks, the 503e RCC was the pride of the French Army. The reality was that the Roanne plant was producing very slowly and had delivered the last of the 503e RCC's 54 tanks only a month previously.

Between 1967 and 1970 the introduction of the new tank proceeded into the training establishment at Saumur and Canjuers, and to the armoured regiments. The second regiment equipped was the 501e RCC in 1968, but only some 10 to 15 tanks per month could be completed at the *Atelier de Roanne*, so each regiment receiving the new tank kept M47 Pattons on strength for up to a year during the transition. Quantity production really began in 1970-71 with some 190-200 vehicles built each year thereafter, earlier production having focused exclusively on gun tanks. What this meant to the units equipped with the M47 in the *Forces Francaises en Allemagne* (FFA) in West Germany was that complete re-equipment took far longer than had ever been anticipated in 1963 when the order to produce the vehicle was tentatively given.

The crews are wearing web gear and their green combat uniforms. Exercises like *EXTEL Crevecoeur* were held every autumn for much of the AMX-30B's service during the cold war. The simulator gear midway down the top of the gun barrel on the tank on the left is evident. [C. Legrand]

Seen here mainly in the blue overalls issued for wear during maintenance, these tanks crews of the *2/501e RCC* are at rest. The use of mud as a temporary camouflage was widespread prior to the adoption of the NATO 3-tone camouflage pattern. [C. Legrand]

By 1988 the 501e RCC had adopted the 3-tone NATO camouflage scheme. This photo taken in October 1988 during *EXTEL Demeter* shows a line up of AMX-30B tanks, possibly awaiting transporters. [C. Legrand]

The armoured divisional structure at the time of the AMX-30's adoption was the *Division 1967*, based on a three brigade organization. While in theory these were all supposed to be *brigades mécanisées* with a regiment each of AMX-30B, in reality some divisions had to employ a *brigade motorisée*, which employed a *régiment blindé* of AMX-13 light tanks, as the third component brigade due to budgetary reasons. With the AMX-30B entering service more slowly than expected, the M47 remained part of the equipment of the *régiment blindé* in the *brigades mécanisées*. The M47 did not completely depart from the French armoured divisions until 1973. It would be the mid-1980s before retirement in the case of the AMX-13, which remained in service in mechanised infantry regiments and in infantry divisions. Priority for deliveries of the new AMX-30B in the 1970s (and for its subsequent modernization) was generally accorded to the FFA armoured units, at the expense of the armoured divisions of the two army corps based in metropolitan France.

Marked with a red air recognition pannel on its gun barrel for the exercise, this 2e Escadron AMX-30B crosses over a pontoon trackway at Mailly in October 1988. [C. Legrand]

In spite of the economic realities of the situation the defence press and government gave much positive publicity to the arrival of the new AMX-30B. The early 1970s were a tough time economically for France and the oil crisis of 1973 was particularly keenly felt in the army. Several important institutional changes took place in the army (and in the defence industry) in France in the early 1970s to add obstacles to what was already a rough transition into service. Firstly the *Arme Blindée Cavalerie* was established as a formal, united arm of service in 1970 (although the tank and cavalry regiments had since 1942 been administered as a single entity). While this represented a positive move, it also spurred the army's general staff to re-examine how armoured divisions could be organised to reduce operating costs.

The rest of the platoon follows, under the watchful eyes of engineers (or possibly *éclaireurs*) with their Hotchkiss Jeeps. [C. Legrand]

The Berliet GBC 8KT 180 replaced the old GMC trucks received from the USA after the war and served in AMX-30 regiments for years. It formed the basis for the modern GBC 180 truck series built by Renault Trucks. The Jeep we see here is the license built Hotchkiss VLTT M201 version that served the French Army for many years, being replaced in the 1990s by the Peugeot P4. The Jeep required dedicated gasoline tanks on each base, shared at first with the AMX-13 carriers, but otherwise the lone vehicles powered by gasoline in what became a diesel only army. [Thomas Seignon]

The Peugeot P4 replaced the Hotchkiss M201 in turn in the 1990s and was basically a Mercedes G series vehicle built under license in France. The vehicle seen here is being used by the army chief of the general staff and the general commanding the *10e Division Blindée* in 1985. The AMX-30s belong to the *4e Régiment de Dragons*. The P4 was also used as the standard recce vehicle in the Escadrons d'Eclairage Divisionnaire (EED), the divisional reconnaissance team. The EED were drawn from the cavalry and were usually based with one of the armoured division's armoured regiments. The P4 could carry a 7.62mm machine gun or a MILAN missile. This P4 was from EED 10, based at Mourmelon with the 503e RCC and the 4e RD throughout the 1980s. [Thomas Seignon]

The AMX-30B was the first French Army battle tank equipped to be able to operate in an NBC environment. Actual operations in an NBC environment were regularly practised during the training year. Here an AMX-30B tank of the *501e RCC* is being decontaminated by chemical troops in full NBC gear in the autumn of 1989. [C. Legrand]

The AMX-30B was a vehicle designed to operate in the toxic environment of chemical or nuclear war. The nature of an NBC exercise could mean being closed in for many hours, a highly unpleasant environment for the crew. Here we see the happy moment when the turret was opened up again. [D. Rotaris]

The *Division Blindée 1977* was the ultimate result of this process, an armoured division that dispensed with subordinate brigades and thus simplified the divisional command structure. This new division organization was designed around nuclear capability and the capabilities of the new AMX-30 family. The refinement of the armoured divisions' basic organization had

therefore been implemented twice within eleven years, largely an admission that the *Division 1967* template was too expensive for the nation's budget.

In 1973 the French government also reformed the land defence industry to create a more efficient system for arms production. This evolution was necessary because the *Direction*

1977: *Bethune* of the *1e Régiment de Cuirassiers* showing the typical markings worn by the regiment until the mid-1980s. [Paul Baron]

A sunken road on the training area at Mailly during the muddy autumn of 1989. The Champagne area of eastern France was used for annual maneuvers for many years, and this is a fitting picture of the AMX-30's natural habitat. [C. Legrand]

This AMX-30B of 3ᵉ Escadron of the 6ᵉ Régiment de Dragons is equipped with a SIMFIRE fire simulator fixed on top of the main gun barrel. This system was used in preference to firing 105mm blank rounds, which were never distributed in large numbers because of the dangers it posed to nearby troops (and its tendency to dirty the main gun barrel in a very severe fashion !), despite the fact that blanks offered the loader a more realistic training regimen. [Thomas Seignon]

January 1989 with the 501e RCC, *Austerlitz,* still in *vert armée,* moving at speed with rangefinders open, thus possibly on a battle run at the firing ranges. [C. Legrand]

Technique des Armaments Terrestres bureau (or DTAT, as DEFA had been re-named) was a massive bureaucratic organization with many old establishments under its umbrella. It needed to be streamlined for economic reasons, and as a part of this process the creation of a nationalised land armaments company took place. This one company replaced the host of government arsenals with their own administrations controlled by one government bureau. A single nationally owned company was now tasked with the state's research, development and production of heavy weapon systems for land warfare. The heir itself of DEFA, the *Direction-Technologique des Armaments Terrestres* (DTAT) became the state armaments company known as *Groupement Industriel des Arméments Terrestres,* or GIAT.

GIAT had to modernise its organization as quickly as possible to be competitive in a changing market, but it could not evolve so quickly that arms production would be affected. GIAT was also

Normandie, an AMX-30B of the *501e RCC* at rest during maneuvers in 1986. The locally applied mud camouflage disrupter is in evidence. [C. Legrand]

Eylau of the *501e RCC* during refueling in 1986, with the shell loading hatch in the turret side open. [C. Legrand]

Two tanks of the *1e Escadron, 501e RCC* in 1987. The tank on the left side is stowed to regulations, with large bags of crew kit stowed on top of the turret rear bin. [C. Legrand]

Mud was used extensively as a temporary disrupter over the overall *Vert Armée* paint job with which all AMX-30Bs left the factory at Roanne. The crewmembers shown here in 1987 wear the canvas webbing introduced with the FAMAS assault rifle. [C. Legrand]

The *Escadron de Commande et Logistique* (ECL) was the command apparatus of the AMX-30 regiment, equivalent to a Headquarters Squadron in a British Armoured Regiment. A wide variety of armoured and soft-skinned vehicles were required in the support roles necessary for the function of an AMX-30 regiment. The Unimog pictured here is set up as a command vehicle with the LA27 antenna used in the regimental command net. The Unimog generally equipped FFA armoured regiments, while the SUMB BH600 (SUMB being SIMCA Unic Marmon Bocquet, but normally shortened to *Marmon*) was used in units stationed in France. [Thomas Seignon]

under pressure to sell and export weapon systems to defray its own operating costs, which were completely bankrolled by the French taxpayer. As far as the AMX-30 series was concerned, with the gun tank in production, GIAT's focus shifted to the development of the sophisticated artillery variants on the AMX-30 chassis required for the *Division 1977*, the advanced AMX-10P infantry fighting vehicle and the AMX-10RC armoured car. Since these systems included the development of a complex self-propelled medium artillery system and even more technologically complex launcher vehicles for surface to air and surface to surface missiles, the further development of the standard AMX-30B for the French Army was not pursued beyond component improvement for the rest of the 1970s. While further development of the basic AMX-30B by GIAT was always an option, the French army could not fund an improved battle tank until 1980.

The ECL also used armoured personnel carriers as command vehicles, normally deployed with the regimental command headquarters. The AMX-13 VTT PC (*Poste de Commande*) was equipped with additional radio equipment and was normally armed with a 12.7mm heavy machine gun, not mounted in the example seen here. This AMX-13VTT PC served in this capacity until the late 1970s. [Thomas Seignon]

The VCI AMX10P which replaced the AMX-13 VTT was also employed as a command vehicle. Each regiment had two AMX-10PCs in the post 1984 organization, all other command vehicles being based on VABs. The PC version of the AMXP had an electronics module fitted to the rear of the hull between the smoke dischargers. The turret is in the 9 o'clock position and with ejected cases visible, we can see that the vehicle was photographed during a range period. [Thomas Seignon]

The AMX-30's Early Regimental Service

The AMX-30B was first deployed in 54 tank regiments in the 1967 type armoured divisions. The composition of French armoured regiments and armoured squadrons changed during the service life of the AMX-30B and its derivatives, with the major changes coming at regimental level between 1967 and 1970 for the type's introduction and again in 1984. In the early 1990s the regimental organization changed once more to follow the pattern expected for the new Leclerc.

The reorganization of each armoured regiment to the Division 1967 pattern envisioned for the AMX-30 was implemented from 1966 onwards, although as we have seen the M47 remained in service while sufficient AMX-30 tanks were built. The small annual production per year between 1966 and 1970 naturally meant that AMX-30B regiments were equipped at first only partially. Tactical procedures for the new tank were developed during this early period. The *503e Regiment de Chars de Combat*, fully equipped by mid-1967, afterwards specialised in submerged crossings in order to set the various associated

The VAB (Véhicule de l'Avant Blindé) was also adapted as a command vehicle. With the AMX-10P the VAB formed the basis of the AMX-30 regiment's command apparatus between the late 1970s and the 21st Century. Each regiment maintained two command groups each formed around an AMX-30 command tank, a VAB PC and an AMX-10P PC to ensure a backup command apparatus was available. [Thomas Seignon]

Troops of the 501e RCC's *Escadron Porté* showing a variety of kit and weaponry in 1981. The rifles are the 7.5mm MAS 49/56 semiautomatic rifle introduced in the late 1950s, the submachine guns are the distinctive MAT-49. Individual equipment at the time was still a mixture of leather and canvas webbing. The style of olive green uniform shown was worn from the late 1960s until the early 1990s, replacing the *tenue camouflage lézard* in the years immediately before the introduction of the AMX-30B. The organic infantrymen in French armoured regiments received new weapons like the 5.56mm FAMAS assault rifle later than infantry units, and often served in auxiliary roles in the day to day workings of the regiment. In the *501e RCC* many of the *éclaireurs* of the *escadron porté* were bandsmen. [C. Legrand]

The FAMAS assault rifle, which began to be issued in 1977-78 to infantry units, made its appearance in the *régiments blindés* in the 1981-1983 period. It became the standard crew weapon on the AMX-30 series battle tanks, replacing the MAT-49. [C. Legrand]

An AMX10P of the 501e RCC taken in 1979 during exercises. [C. Legrand]

An AMX-10P photographed at Rambouillet in 1981. The AMX-10P was introduced into the *régiments blindées* in 1977-1979, and replaced the more lightly armed AMX-13VTT. It served as the AMX30B's main support vehicle until the mid-1980s, when the VAB replaced the AMX-10P in the armoured regiments of the Division 1984 and the latter were handed over to the RIMECA (or mechanized infantry). [C. Legrand]

Smolensk: the 11e *Régiment de Chasseurs* were the French armoured regiment stationed in Berlin, seen here next to a Queen's Own Hussars Chieftain in 1983. The two tanks make a very interesting contrast in how NATO nations prioritised design features in the main battle tank designs of the 1960s. We can also see the turret roof layout of the AMX-30B. [Justin Steadman]

procedures and training methods. The *5e Régiment de Cuirassiers* received their AMX-30Bs in spring 1969, having adopted 1967 regimental organization in July 1968 while still equipped with the Patton. The 2e Cuirassiers received the AMX-30 in 1971, having changed to the new regimental structure in 1969. While nearly all of the French tank regiments adopted the 1967 structure at about the same time, the AMX-30Bs that were to equip them did not arrive in some cases until 1972-73.

In the Division 1967's *régiment blindé* (armoured regiment), four of five *escadrons* (squadrons) were supposed to be composed of thirteen AMX-30B tanks each (with one command tank with two AMX-13 VTT carriers in the command section and four *pelotons*, platoons, of three tanks each). Two more battle tanks were at regimental headquarters. The fifth squadron, known as the *escadron porté* was composed of twelve AMX-13 VTT carrying mounted infantry, organised as

The AMX-13VTT served as the AMX-30 regiment's armoured ambulance for forward casualty evacuation from the 1970s until the late 1980s, when it was replaced by the VAB Sanitaire. [Thomas Seignon]

The Renault R2067 4x4 ambulance was a simple adaption of the civilian 4x2 version, and served in French armoured regiments until the 1980s. It could carry 4 stretcher casualties. [Thomas Seignon]

In the 1980s the VAB Sanitaire took over the AMX-13VTT's armoured ambulance role in French armoured regiments. [Thomas Seignon]

Tanks of the 4e RC crossing a river in 1980. This AMX-30B descends to the river edge. [P. Besson]

Crossing one behind the other, this fording exercise was undertaken by an entire peloton. [P. Besson]

a mechanised infantry company, again with two more AMX-13 VTT command vehicles at headquarters level. The organic infantry component could be used as a complete company or as detached sections in each tank squadron as situations required.

The 1967 pattern *division mecanisée*, employed a three brigade structure. Within each *brigade mecanisée* there were two *régiments mecanisés* and one *régiment blindé* supported by a medium self-propelled artillery regiment (equipped with 155mm self-propelled guns on AMX-13 chassis). Each French army infantry division also included an armoured regiment, which for the early period of the AMX-30B's service retained the AMX-13 light tank armed with the CN 90 F-3 90mm gun or earlier 75mm gun and SS11 missiles. At the beginning of

the 1970s AMX-30B production was only sufficient to re-equip three regiments per year.

The next round of changes brought about by the 1977 re-organization of the French army involved the elimination of brigades and several regiments from the French order of battle, and the redistribution of a number of infantry regiments. It did not change the regimental organization employed by the *regiment blindé*. By the mid-1980s, with sufficient AMX-30B tanks in service to employ them outside of the *divisions blindées,* the AMX-30B also began to replace the AMX-13 in the mechanised infantry regiments that formed the infantry components of each *division blindé.* By the middle of the 1970s the AMX-30B was the army's standard battle tank, with over 1000 gun tanks available by the dawn of the 1980s.

An atmospheric view of one of the Saone bridges taken for the commanding officer of the 4e RC. Notice how the towing ropes are rigged for recovery prior to entry into the water. [P. Besson]

An AMX-30B of the Hellenic Army's XXII Armoured Brigade, XX Armoured Division, photographed parading through the Greek capital of Athens March 25th 1984, Greek National Independence Day. [Triantafyllos Metsovitis]

Hellenic Army's AMX-30Bs were delivered in overall *Vert Armée* but like the army's M48 tanks, they received a camouflage paint scheme in subsequent years. [Triantafyllos Metsovitis]

Sand shields were an option first seen as standard issue on the Greek AMX-30Bs, which comprised the first foreign order for the type in 1969. They were all delivered by 1973. [Triantafyllos Metsovitis]

AMX-30 Units and Formations 1966 to 1993: Arme Blindée Cavalerie (Including AMX-30B2)

Régiment (Arme Blindée Cavalrie)	Brigade (1967)	Division Mécanisée (Type 1967)	Division Blindée (Type 1977)	Year Equipped with AMX30B	Division Blindées 1984	after 1990
1e Régiment de Cuirassiers	1e Brigade Mécanisée	1e Division Mécanisée	1e Division Blindée	1969 RC54	1e Division Blindée (RC70)	amalgamated with 11e Regiment de Cuirassiers 1999 (RC80)
501e Régiment de Chars de Combat	2e Brigade Mécanisée	8e Division Mécanisée	2e Division Blindée	1967-1968 RC54	2e Division Blindée	amalgamated with 503e Regiment de Chars de Combat 1994 (RC80)
5e Régiment de Cuirassiers	3e Brigade Mécanisée	1e Division Mécanisée	5e Division Blindée	1969 RC54	5e Division Blindée	dissolved in 1992
7e Régiment de Cuirassiers	4e Brigade Mécanisée	8e Division Mécanisée (in lieu of régiment blindé)		7eRC never received AMX30, remained an EBR regiment,	NA	NA
2e Régiment de Cuirassiers	5e Brigade Mécanisée	3e Division Mécanisée	5e Division Blindée	1971 RC54	5e Division Blindée	dissolved in 1991
2e Régiment de Dragons	6e Brigade Mécanisée	7e Division Mécanisée	6e Division Blindée	1970 RC54	2e Division Blindée	Last regiment (1994) equipped with AMX-30-B, ABC NBC regiment as of 2005
30e Régiment de Dragons	7e Brigade Mécanisée	7e Division Mécanisée	dissolved in Sept 1978	1968 RC54		
3e Régiment de Cuirassiers	8e Brigade Mécanisée	7e Division Mécanisée	4e Division Blindée	1973 RC54	7e Division Blindée	dissolved in 1998
503e Régiment de Chars de Combat	10e Brigade Mécanisée	4e Division Mécanisée	10e Division Blindée	1966-1967 RC54	10e Division Blindée	amalgamated with 501e Regiment de Chars de Combat 1994
6e Régiment de Dragons	11e Brigade Mécanisée	1e Division Mécanisée	1e Division Blindée	1972 RC54	1e Division Blindée	dissolved in 1992
12e Régiment de Cuirassiers	12e Brigade Mécanisée	3e Division Mécanisée	3e Division Blindée	1970? RC54	3e Division Blindée	amalgamated with 6e Regiment de Cuirassiers 1994 (RC80)
5e Régiment de Hussards	13e Brigade Mécanisée	3e Division Mécanisée (in lieu of régiment blindé)	dissolved in Dec 1975 became 3e Dragons January 1976	never got AMX30, EBR regiment until 1975 and then received AMX-30 as 3eRD	NA	NA
6e Régiment de Cuirassiers	14e Brigade Mécanisée	8e Division Mécanisée	2e Division Blindée	1970 RC54	2e Division Blindée	amalgamated with 12e Regiment de Cuirassiers 1994 (RC80)
2e Régiment de Chasseurs	15e Brigade Mécanisée	4e Division Mécanisée	4e Division Blindée	1970? RC54	10e Division Blindée	amalgamated with 1e Regiment de Chasseurs 1998 (RC80 Brennus)
4e Régiment de Cuirassiers	16e Brigade Mécanisée	4e Division Mécanisée	6e Division Blindée	1970 RC54	5e Division Blindée (RC70 in 1992)	dissolved in 1997
507e Regiment de Chars de Combat	Saumur Training Regiment	Saumur Training Regiment	Saumur Training Regiment	1968? partial equipment on training establishment	12e Division Légère Blindée	dissolved in 1997
1e Régiment de Dragons	NA	NA	7e Division Blindée	1981? RC54	7e Division Blindée	dissolved in 1997
5e Régiment de Dragons	NA	formed from 30e Dragons 1978-79	7e Division Blindée	1978 RC54 (renamed 30e RD)	7e Division Blindée (1994-1997 with 27e DI de Montagne, then returned to 7e DB)	became RC70 with AMX30B2 received in 1992, dissolved 2003.
4e Régiment de Dragons	NA	NA	10e Division Blindée	1981? RC54	10e Division Blindée	dissolved in 1994 after service in Operation Daguet
11e Régiment de Cuirassiers	NA	NA	NA	1981? RC54	14e Division Légère Blindée	amalgamated with 1e Regiment de Cuirassiers 1999 (RC80)
1e Régiment de Chasseurs	NA	NA	NA	1976 AMX-30B, partial re-equipment with AMX-30B2 after 1981.	14e Division Légère Blindée	amalgamated with 2e Regiment de Chasseurs 1996 (RC80 Brennus)
3e Régiment de Chasseurs	NA	NA	NA	recreated 1981 RC54	12e Division Légère Blindée	dissolved in 1997
11e Régiment de Chasseurs	NA	NA	NA	1981 RC54	Forces Francaises a Berlin	dissolved 1994
3e Régiment de Dragons	NA	NA	3e Division Blindée	1976 RC54	3e Division Blindée	dissolved in 1997
		1967 system: 5 Divisions Mécanisées in two Corps d'Armée	1977 System: 8 Divisions Blindées in three Corps d'Armée	Approximate number of tanks in service by 1986: 1200 in ABC (including 200 AMX-30B2)	1984 System: 6 Divisions Blindées and 2 Divisions Légères Blindées in three Corps d'Armée plus 1 DLB in the Force d'Action Rapide	

AMX-30B in the Infanterie Mécanisée 1982 to 1993

Régiments d'Infanterie Mécanisé	Division Blindé (1984)	FFA or FRANCE Metropole	year equipped with AMX 30B	probable number of tanks
8e Groupe de Chasseurs	1e Division Blindée	FFA	1982-1986	2 compagnies or 1 escadron (max 16)
16e Groupe de Chasseurs	1e Division Blindée	FFA	1982-1986	2 compagnies or 1 escadron (max 16)
5e Régiment d'Infanterie	2e Division Blindée	FRANCE	after 1985	1 compagnie (10 tanks)
Régiment de Marche du Tchad	2e Division Blindée	FRANCE	after 1985	1 compagnie (10 tanks)
19e Groupe de Chasseurs	3e Division Blindée	FFA	1982-1986	2 compagnies or 1 escadron (max 16)
42e Régiment d'Infanterie	3e Division Blindée	FFA	1982-1986	2 compagnies or 1 escadron (max 16)
2e Groupe de Chasseurs	4e Division Blindée	FFA	1982-1986	2 compagnies or 1 escadron (max 16)
24e Groupe de Chasseurs	4e Division Blindée	FFA	1982-1986	2 compagnies or 1 escadron (max 16)
35e Régiment d'Infanterie	7e Division Blindée	FRANCE	after 1985	1 compagnie (10 tanks)
170e Régiment d'Infanterie	7e Division Blindée	FRANCE	after 1985	1 compagnie (10 tanks)
1e Groupe de Chasseurs	10e Division Blindée	FRANCE	after 1985	1 compagnie (10 tanks)
150e Régiment d'Infanterie	10e Division Blindée	FRANCE	after 1985	1 compagnie (10 tanks)
3e Régiment d'Infanterie*	14e Division Légère Blindée	FRANCE	after 1985	maximum of 12 tanks

* Training Regiment, incomplete equipment

Potential Number of AMX-30B tanks in RIMECA by 1991: 182-200 vehicles

AMX-30 Markings

From the 1950s until 1986-1987 French tanks were identified by a 3-digit numbering system painted on the rear face of the turret bustle bin (M47 and AMX-30B). These numbers were used for the 1967 *Regiment Blindé* and for the RIMECA *Compagnie de Chars*. The numbers were either solid or hollow but were nearly always painted in white.

The first digit (1-5) denoted the **Escadron** (ABC) or **Compagnie** (RIMECA)
The second digit (0,1,2,3,4,5) denoted the **Peloton** (ABC) or **Section** (RIMECA) within the **Escadron** or **Compagnie**
The third digit (0,1,2,3,4,5) denoted the tank within the **Peloton** (ABC) or **Section** (RIMECA).

A geometric turret marking system was introduced after 1986 in the 1984 pattern *Régiment de Chars* and was also adopted by the RIMECA. These symbols were painted in lower visibility gray and represented an effort to ensure that a potential enemy would have a harder time identifying command vehicles or different sub-units on the battlefield. The 3 colour NATO camouflage pattern was adopted at around the same time.

✕✕ Regimental Commander
✕ Second in Command
■ 1e Escadron/Compagnie
● 2e Escadron/Compagnie
▲ 3e Escadron/Compagnie
◆ 4e Escadron/Compagnie

To the right of the *Escadron* or *Compagnie* Marking the *Peloton* or *Section* was denoted by solid vertical bars. An *Escadron* or *Compagnie* command tank was only marked with the geometric symbol. The *Peloton* or *Section* commander's tank would show only the *Escadron/ Compagnie* Geometric marking followed by the number of vertical bars denoting the correct *Peloton* or *Section*.

| 1e Peloton

|| 2e Peloton

||| 3e Peloton

|||| 4e Peloton

The position of the tank within the Peloton or Section was indicated by a horizontal bar under the Peloton/Section marking:
Example:

▲ |||| would be 3 Esc, 4 Pl command tank

▲ |||| would be 3 Esc, 4 Pl, 2nd in command

▲ |||| would be 3 Esc, 4 Pl, 3rd tank

▲ |||| would be 3 Esc, 4 Pl, 4th tank

AMX-30B Escadron Type 1967 with turret numbers

Peloton de Commandement

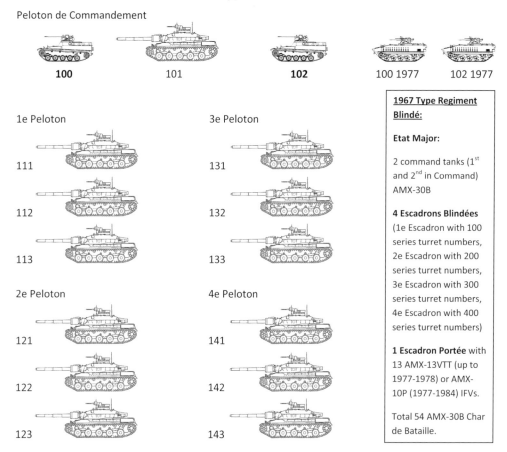

100 101 **102** 100 1977 102 1977

1e Peloton

111

112

113

3e Peloton

131

132

133

2e Peloton

121

122

123

4e Peloton

141

142

143

1967 Type Regiment Blindé:

Etat Major:

2 command tanks (1st and 2nd in Command) AMX-30B

4 Escadrons Blindées (1e Escadron with 100 series turret numbers, 2e Escadron with 200 series turret numbers, 3e Escadron with 300 series turret numbers, 4e Escadron with 400 series turret numbers)

1 Escadron Portée with 13 AMX-13VTT (up to 1977-1978) or AMX-10P (1977-1984) IFVs.

Total 54 AMX-30B Char de Bataille.

REGIMENT 1984: 501e Régiment de Chars de Combat

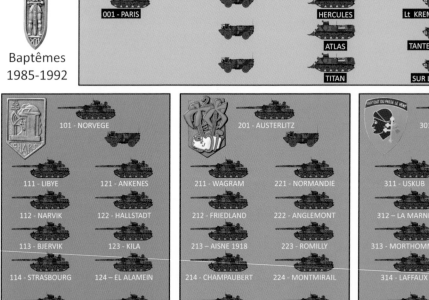

Baptêmes 1985-1992

001 - PARIS   HERCULES   Lt KREMENCHOUSKY
ATLAS   TANTE MIRABELLE
TITAN   SUR LE CHAMPS

101 - NORVEGE

111 - LIBYE   121 - ANKENES
112 - NARVIK   122 - HALLSTADT
113 - BJERVIK   123 - KILA
114 - STRASBOURG   124 – EL ALAMEIN
131 - MEDENINE   141 - MOURZOUK
132 - EL OUTID   142 - KOUFRA
133 - HIMEIMAT   143 - MASSAOUA
134 – KSAR HILANE 144 - KEREN

201 - AUSTERLITZ

211 - WAGRAM   221 - NORMANDIE
212 - FRIEDLAND   222 - ANGLEMONT
213 - AISNE 1918   223 - ROMILLY
214 - CHAMPAUBERT 224 - MONTMIRAIL
231 - IENA   241 - LUTZEN
232 - EYLAU   242 - BAUTZEN
233 - ULM   243 - ECKMUHL
234 – LA MOSKOWA   244 - ECOUCHE

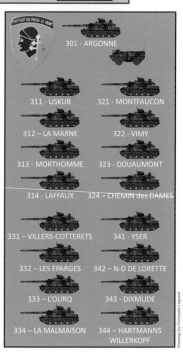

301 - ARGONNE

311 - USKUB   321 - MONTFAUCON
312 – LA MARNE   322 - VIMY
313 - MORTHOMME   323 - DOUAUMONT
314 - LAFFAUX   324 – CHEMIN des DAMES
331 – VILLERS-COTTERETS 341 - YSER
332 – LES EPARGES 342 - N-D DE LORETTE
333 – L'OURQ   343 - DIXMUDE
334 – LA MALMAISON 344 – HARTMANNS WILLERKOPF

The AMX-30B employed a conventional suspension with 5 large road wheels on each side, a front mounted idler and a rear mounted sprocket. [Pierre Delattre]

The front pair of roadwheel axle arms were mounted with the front arm leading and the rear wheel trailing. The torsion bars that sprung these arms ran perpendicular through the hull. A large shock absorber was mounted on top of the front suspension unit. This system was known in France as the Vickers system. [Pierre Delattre]

The second suspension unit was mounted at a point just over two thirds down the chassis. Like the front unit, it featured paired leading and trailing axle arms, with torsion bars running through the hull width. The middle unit did not require a shock absorber. [Pierre Delattre]

The sprocket, aft return roller and final drive. [Pierre Delattre]

The rearmost roadwheel was sprung on a leading axle arm. A prominent bump stop was mounted over each axle arm. It was linked to a shock absorber. [Pierre Delattre]

A closeup of the middle suspension unit showing the axle arm mounts and the return roller. [Pierre Delattre]

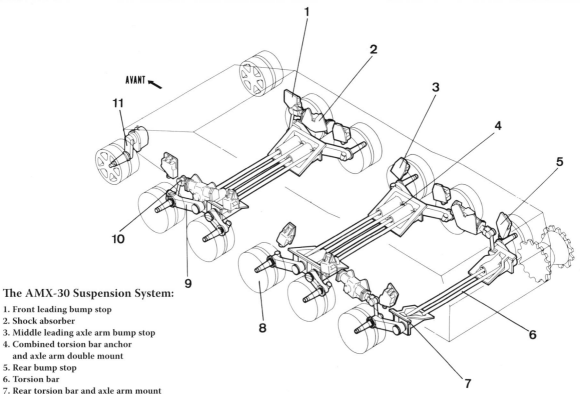

AVANT

The AMX-30 Suspension System:

1. Front leading bump stop
2. Shock absorber
3. Middle leading axle arm bump stop
4. Combined torsion bar anchor
   and axle arm double mount
5. Rear bump stop
6. Torsion bar
7. Rear torsion bar and axle arm mount
8. Road wheel
9. Axle arm
10. Shock absorber linkage
11. Idler wheel

[Thomas Seignon]

The AMX-30B turret employed an external cover between the mantlet and the turret casting to prevent the ingress of dust and rain. Here we can see it secured with a simple bolt and nut arrangement. The mantlet was a well shaped casting some 79mm thick. [Pierre Delattre]

The commander's cupola machine gun was provided with a removeable brushguard, essential for travel through wooded areas. It attached to the right side rangefinder head and to a mount welded to the edge of the turret roof. [Pierre Delattre]

The right front of the turret and mantlet. Besides the main sight cover, we can see the commander's searchlight and optics, the Top7 cupola, one of the rangefinder heads with its armoured cover, and the cupola machine gun's brush guard. [Pierre Delattre]

The gun mantlet seen from the right side, the gunner's main telescopic sight was provided with a simple hinged cover. The bellows that covered the gun runout was attached with a large bolted ring directly to the mantlet face. We can see the sleeve that once held a *20mm Canon F2*. [Pierre Delattre]

The left side of the mantlet incoporated a separately elevating co-axial armament capable of high angle fire. On early production AMX-30B tanks this would be a 12.7mm machinegun not much different from the venerable M2 Browning. This vehicle also has no PH-8B searchlight so we can see the mounting point. The PH-8B was removable and was stowed on top of the turret bustle stowage bin when not mounted on the gun mantlet. [Pierre Delattre]

The sleeve for the 20mm Canon F2 with the PH-8B searchlight fitted. [Pierre Delattre]

The original pattern 12.7mm co-axial machine gun mount seen from the side. The PH-8B mount and the loader's periscope optics are also visible. [Pierre Delattre]

The PH-8B was a dual infra red and white light searchlight typical of those fitted to the NATO MBTs developed in the 1960s and it endured on the AMX-30B2 right into the late 1990s despite its obsolesence. The projector doors opened outwards and could be opened or closed from inside the turret. [Pierre Delattre]

The PH-8B shown is missing its electrical operating cables but otherwise is complete. Behind it we can see the left side rangefinder head and one of the loader's fixed episcopes. Although this would technically have weakened the turret wall, the design philosophy of the AMX-30B valued observation, firepower and speed over armoured protection. [Pierre Delattre]

The PH-8B from the rear. We can see the rear access cover held in place with a large cap, and at the top right of the projector box we can see the plug-ins for the power cables. On the turret wall we can see the corresponding outlet point on the extreme right of the photo. This preserved vehicle lacks the dust cover between the mantlet and the turret body seen on operational vehicles. [Pierre Delattre]

A closeup of the cable mounts and the attachment bracket for the dust cover behind the searchlight mount. [Pierre Delattre]

The electical power outlet and rangefinder head on the left sid eof the turret casting. The rangefinder heads had armoured covers that opened downwards. The white disc and two red circular markings are the standard SNCF rail weight classification markings. This type of marking changed from the mid 1960s, when a simple white bar was painted in the same position, to a white disc with a 5 painted inside, to the pattern seen here. [Pierre Delattre]

A general view of the left side of the vehicle, with loader's episcopes and track pad stowage visible. [Pierre Delattre]

The TOP7 cupola and the gunner's fixed episcope. The TOP7 had 10 M268 episcopes and was a feature that was well liked by its crews for the excellent battlefield view it offered. [Pierre Delattre]

The right side of the turret showing the cupola and the cradle for the ANF-1 7.62mm machine gun. [Pierre Delattre]

The rangefinder head seen from the side. [Pierre Delattre]

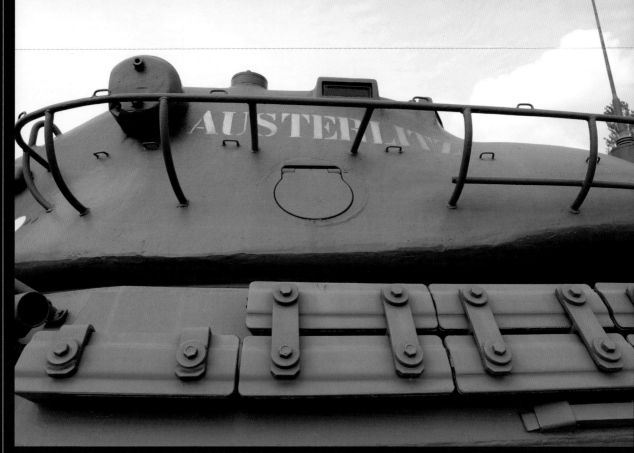

The left side of the turret also incorporated a loading hatch for the rapid stowage of ammunition and for removing spent cases from the turret. [Pierre Delattre]

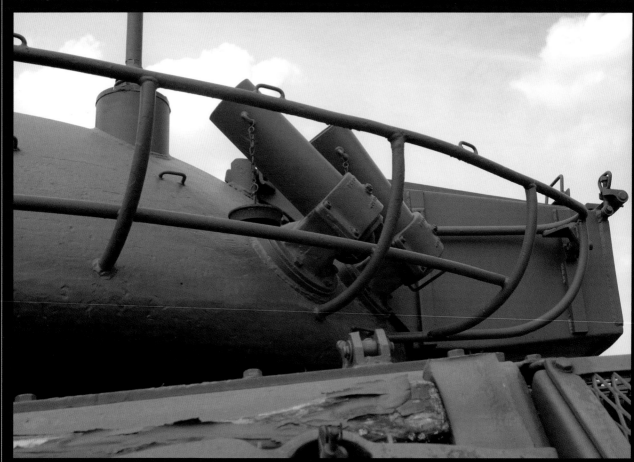

On each side of the turret rear were two forward facing smoke dischargers. [Pierre Delattre]

The turret bustle bin held stowage items and incorporated part of the NBC filtration system. We can also see the mounts for the smoke dischargers, which are bolted into plates welded to the turret casting. [Pierre Delattre]

The commander's searchlight and the ANF-1 cradle with its associated Bowden cables, which allowed the machinegun to be fired from inside the cupola. [Pierre Delattre]

The AMX-30B had a very cluttered hull exterior. Here we can see the running lights, two battery compartment covers, the empty fire extinguisher brackets and the empty tow rope attachment brackets. The brushguards once held infrared lamps on the inside positions. The outer edge sections of the glacis actually conceal a stowage box on each hull side. [Pierre Delattre]

The driver's position was actually a separately fabricated assembly that was welded into the casting that made up the hull front. It included 3 periscopes, the central one being removeable. An infra red periscope could be fitted for night driving, an arrangement later modernised during the AMX-30B2 program to incorporate an image intensifying device for the driver instead. [Pierre Delattre]

The right hand headlamp assembly. [Pierre Delattre]

AMX-30B Glacis and Front Hull Stowage

1. Wire cutter post
2. Mirror
3. Indicator
4. Black out lamp
5. Headlamp
6. Infrared lamp
7. CO2 Fire extinguisher
8. Siren

[Thomasa Seignon]

On the left side of the hull we can see the door for the stowage box and behind it we can see the vent for the crew heater and the pull handle for the fixed fire extinguishers. [Pierre Delattre]

We can make out the small size of the front stowage box on the right side of the hull front with the fire extinguisher brackets mounted on top. [Pierre Delattre]

This vehicle, preserved on the base of the 501e-503e RCC in 2003, has a very complete exterior stowage set. We can see how the tow rope and fire extinguishers are stowed and the drivers periscope optics. [Pierre Delattre]

A closeup of the driver's hatch. [Pierre Delattre]

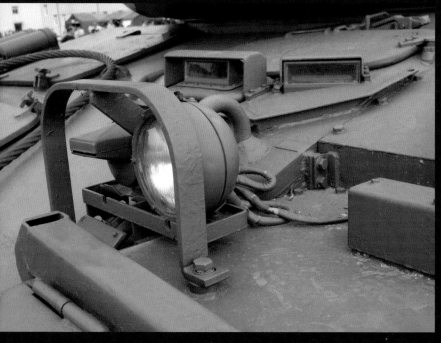

The left hand headlamp cluster with brushguard. [Pierre Delattre]

The left hand headlamp cluster seen from the front. [Pierre Delattre]

The drivers position seen from the left hand side. [Pierre Delattre]

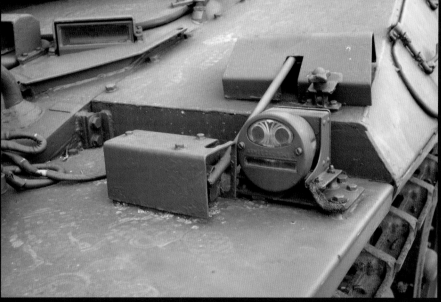

On top of the left front stowage box we see the driver's mirror in the stowed position and the running light. [Pierre Delattre]

The exterior mounted fire extinguishers were mounted in brackets on top of the front right stowage box. [Pierre Delattre]

The right front mudguard with the weight classification disc marked in yellow and black. These bright early markings were replaced by low visibility gray weight discs after the 3 tone barriolage was introduced in the mod 1980s. [Pierre Delattre]

The two hull stowage boxes opened downwards and were secured by 3 large latches. Here we can see the left side stowage box door. [Pierre Delattre]

The AMX-30 series tanks lacked stowage space as a consequence of their compact size, and the left side of the hull held some of the pioneer tools as well as track pads. The tool handles were normally painted Vert Armée along with the tank. [Pierre Delattre]

The mesh covers over the exhaust silencers were a modification made very early in the AMX-30B's career, but were not present on the early production tanks. [Pierre Delattre]

Spare track pads were stowed on the left side of the hull in simple brackets secured by bolts. [Pierre Delattre]

The right rear side of the hull. The prominent exhaust silencers with their hinged covers in the lowered position are visible. One of the most feared problems when deep fording was for the exhaust covers to pop open or not be closed properly, which would immobilise the tank on the river bottom and would require the intervention of the PAFF divers and the best efforts of a recovery team. [Pierre Delattre]

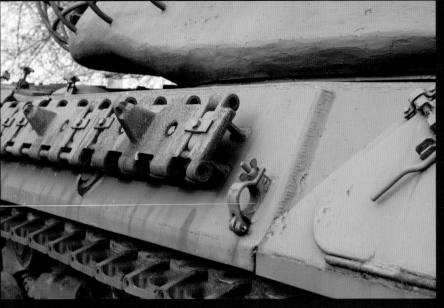

Spare track links were carried on the right side of the hull, secured in a similar method to the spare track pads carried on the opposite side. [Pierre Delattre]

The right side hull stowage bin lid, a mirror image of that on the left side of the hull. [Pierre Delattre]

A closeup of the stowed track links, note the casting numbers. [Pierre Delattre]

Rear view of the rear of the AMX-30B hull. The upper and lower rear plates were detachable for power pack changes and transmission repairs. The two plates also held a variety of stowed equipment. Note the brake lights on the lower corners of the lower rear plate. [Pierre Delattre]

Two jerrycans were stowed on the left side of the upper rear plate. [Pierre Delattre]

Pioneer tools, held in simple steel straps, were carried on the hinged lower rear hull plate. We can see the towing pintle beneath. [Pierre Delattre]

On the left we can see the stowed towing pintle hook, a substantial piece of kit. To its right is the infantry phone box. [Pierre Delattre]

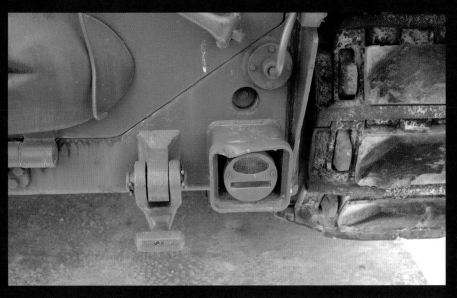

To the left of the brake light we can see the towing point with a bollard hook fitted. The same arrangement was mirrored on the left edge of the lower rear plate. [Pierre Delattre]

We can see the pair of large bolts used to loosen the rear upper plate for removal. Two identical bolts on the opposite side fulfilled the same function. [Pierre Delattre]

Painted by Sławomir Zajączkowski

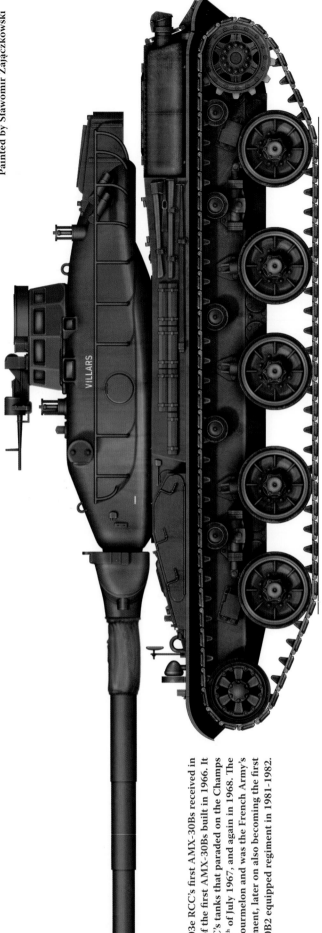

Villars was one the 503e RCC's first AMX-30Bs received in early 1967 and was one of the first AMX-30Bs built in 1966. It was amongst the 503e RCC's tanks that paraded on the Champs Élysée in Paris on the 14ᵗʰ of July 1967, and again in 1968. The 503e RCC was based at Mourmelon and was the French Army's first AMX-30B regiment, later on also becoming the first AMX-30B2 equipped regiment in 1981-1982.

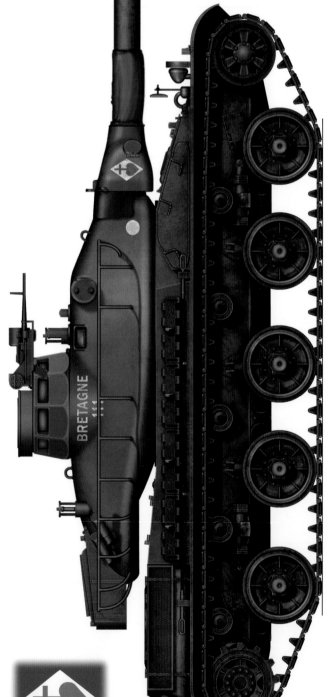

Bretagne was an AMX-30B from the *1e Peloton* of the *1e Escadron, 6e Régiment de Dragons*, seen here in late 1978. The vehicle names in this *escadron* were all after French provinces; the *Croix de Vendée* emblem painted on the mantlet was unique to this peloton and was employed for the duration of its command by *Lieutenant* Fourcade. This goes to show that many platoon level markings within a regiment could be applied at the wishes of individual officers, though not often as boldly as seen here.

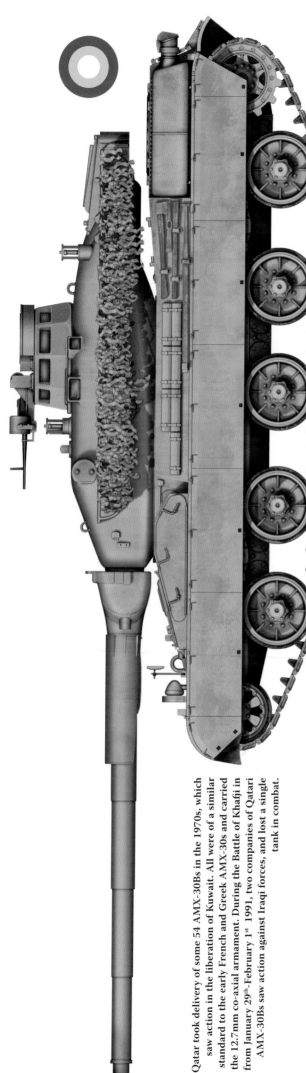

Qatar took delivery of some 54 AMX-30Bs in the 1970s, which saw action in the liberation of Kuwait. All were of a similar standard to the early French and Greek AMX-30s and carried the 12.7mm co-axial armament. During the Battle of Khafji in from January 29th February 1st 1991, two companies of Qatari AMX-30Bs saw action against Iraqi forces, and lost a single tank in combat.

SYL06 *Dunkerque* was a *2e Régiment de Cuirassiers* AMX-30B received in 1971-1972, and carried these markings in 1973. The blue *escadron* markings (inspired by the regiment's wartime markings of 1944-1945) seen on the side were also carried on the front left mudguard and the bottom right corner of the turret bustle stowage box. Turret number was 112.

Painted by Sławomir Zajączkowski

Painted by Sławomir Zajączkowski

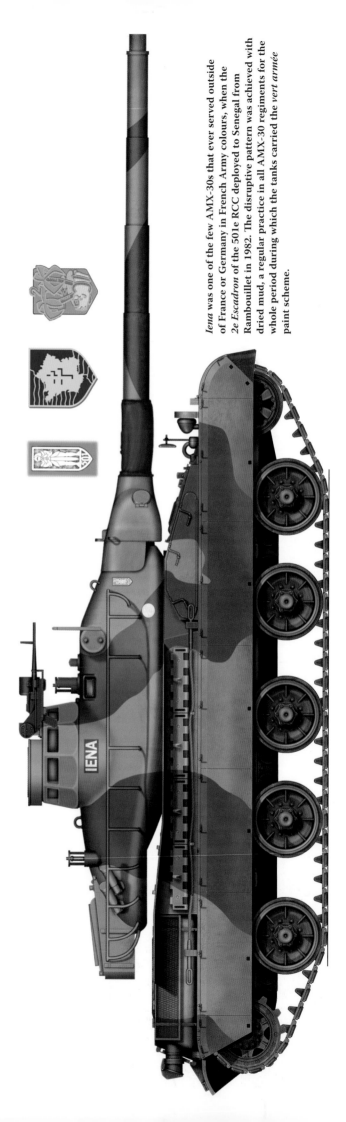

Turenne was the name given to the regimental commander's tank in the *1e Régiment de Cuirassiers*, who received their AMX-30Bs in 1969. The *Maréchal Turenne* was one of France's great military commanders and had served as the 1e RC's first commanding officer. The markings were inherited from the M47s previously by the regiment but disappeared when the 1e RC adopted the 3 tone *barriolage* in the later 1980s, by which time they had re-equipped with AMX-30B2s.

Iena was one of the few AMX-30s that ever served outside of France or Germany in French Army colours, when the *2e Escadron* of the 501e RCC deployed to Senegal from Rambouillet in 1982. The disruptive pattern was achieved with dried mud, a regular practice in all AMX-30 regiments for the whole period during which the tanks carried the *vert armée* paint scheme.

KAGERO.EU

READ FOR FREE on **KAGERO's Area**

LIST OF PUBLICATION SERIES

TopColors

miniTopColors

Units

TopDrawings

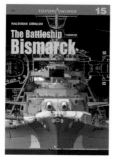

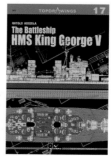
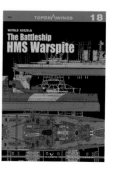

Legends of Aviation

Legends of Aviation in 3D

SuperModel International

SMI Library

Photosniper

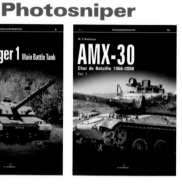

Monographs

Monographs in 3D

Air Battles

Super Drawings in 3D

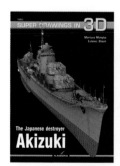
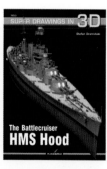
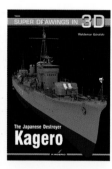
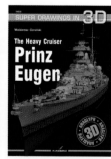

www.shop.kagero.pl
phone +4881 501 21 05